The Technical Guide to Windows™

The Technical Guide to Windows™

Paddy Coleman

Application Development Consultant
Intel Corporation (UK) Ltd.

Adrian Jonathan Cotterill

Development Engineer
Intel Corporation (UK) Ltd.

OXFORD
BLACKWELL SCIENTIFIC PUBLICATIONS
LONDON EDINBURGH BOSTON
MELBOURNE PARIS BERLIN VIENNA

© Paddy Coleman & Adrian Jonathan Cotterill 1992

Blackwell Scientific Publications
Editorial offices:
Osney Mead, Oxford OX2 0EL
25 John Street, London WC1N 2BL
23 Ainslie Place, Edinburgh EH3 6AJ
3 Cambridge Center, Cambridge,
   Massachusetts 02142, USA
54 University Street, Carlton,
   Victoria 3053, Australia

Other Editorial Offices:
Librairie Arnette SA
2, rue Casimir-Delavigne
75006 Paris
France

Blackwell Wissenschafts-Verlag
Meinekestrasse 4
D-1000 Berlin 15
Germany

Blackwell MZV
Feldgasse 13
A-1238 Wien
Austria

First published 1992

Printed and bound in Great Britain by Hartnolls Ltd,
Bodmin, Cornwall

DISTRIBUTORS

Marston Book Services Ltd
PO Box 87
Oxford OX2 0DT
(*Orders*: Tel: 0865 791155
            Fax: 0865 791927
            Telex: 837515)

USA
Blackwell Scientific Publications, Inc.
3 Cambridge Center
Cambridge, MA 02142
(*Orders*: Tel: 800 759–6102
                 617 225–0401)

Canada
Oxford University Press
70 Wynford Drive
Don Mills
Ontario M3C 1J9
(*Orders*: Tel: 416 441–2941)

Australia
Blackwell Scientific Publications
(Australia) Pty Ltd
54 University Street
Carlton, Victoria 3053
(*Orders*: Tel: 03 347–0300)

British Library
Cataloguing in Publication Data

Coleman, Paddy
   The technical guide to Windows.
   I. Title   II. Cotterill, Adrian Jonathan
   005.446

   ISBN 0–632–03374–6

Library of Congress
Cataloging in Publication Data

Coleman, Paddy.
   The technical guide to windows / Paddy
   Coleman, Adrian Jonathan Cotterill.
          p.   cm.
   Includes bibliographical references and index.
   ISBN 0–632–03374–6
   1. Windows (Computer programs)
   2. Microsoft Windows (Computer program)   I.
   Cotterill, Adrian Jonathan.   II. Title.
   QA76.76.W56C65   1992
   005.4'3—dc20   91–40665
                                        CIP

CONTENTS

CONTENTS

PREFACE

Microsoft Windows is a very powerful operating environment for users of DOS systems. This power comes not only in the shape of an intuitive graphical environment but also in its flexibility and configurability.

This book is designed to provide technical information on versions 3.0 and 3.1 of Microsoft Windows. It is written as a practical guide that should help readers understand the technical aspects of their Windows computing environment better, giving them the knowledge needed to be able to make the most of it.

Chapters on installation, operating modes, initialisation files, program information files (PIFs), DOS considerations, memory management, display adaptors and miscellaneous hints and tips cover areas not found in the Microsoft documentation.

If you find this book informative as well as being enjoyable to read then we have succeeded in our aim. We wish you the best with your Windows computing.

ACKNOWLEDGEMENTS

We would like to thank the following people at Intel who contributed to the contents of this book:

Jason Devoys
Stephen Froud
Jon Sharp
Cecil Walker

This book was created electronically using Microsoft Windows Write, with Adobe Type Manager, on Intel486 Business Workstations. Screen images were captured using Windows, tidied up using Windows Paintbrush and resized where necessary using WinGIF. Page layout was done using Microsoft Word for Windows. Final camera ready copy was produced on a Hewlett-Packard LaserJet III printer.

TRADEMARK ACKNOWLEDGEMENTS

Adobe, Adobe Type Manager, ATM, Postscript and TypeAlign are registered trademarks of Adobe Systems Incorporated.
Apple and Macintosh are registered trademarks of Apple Computer, Incorporated.
AutoCAD is a registered trademark of Autodesk, Incorporated.
Banyan is a registered trademark of Banyan Systems, Incorporated.
Sidekick is a registered trademark of Borland International
Compaq is a registered trademark of Compaq Computer Corporation.
Compuserve is a registered trademark of Compuserve Corporation.
Laserjet is a registered trademark of Hewlett-Packard.
IBM, IBM PC, AT, Personal System/2, PS/2, Operating System/2, OS/2,Presentation Manager, MCA, Micro-Channel Architecture, EGA and PC-DOS are registered trademarks of International Business Machines Corporation.
Intel, i, i287, i386, i387, i486, i487, Intel287, Intel386, Intel387, Intel486, Intel487, SnapIn 386, SX, The Computer Inside are registered trademarks of Intel Corporation.
Microsoft, MS, MS DOS, Excel, Windows and Word are registered trademarks of Microsoft Corporation.
Qualitas, 386MAX 5.0, 386MAX 5.1, 386MAX, 386LOAD, 386UTIL and BlueMAX are registered trademarks of Qualitas, Incorporated.
Quarterdeck is a registered trademark of Quarterdeck Office Systems.
Paradise is a registered trademark of Western Digital Corporation.
Ethernet is a registered trademark of Xerox Corporation.
Paintbrush is a registered trademark of Zsoft Corporation.

'The acquisition of any knowledge whatever is always useful to the intellect because it will be able to banish the useless things and retain those which are good. For nothing can either be loved or hated unless it is first known.'

Leonardo Da Vinci (1452-1519).

CHAPTER

1

WINDOWS INSTALLATION

In this chapter we will first of all cover the most common form of Windows installation - placing it on either a stand-alone or networked PC's hard disk. Later we will explain how to install and configure Windows on a network server.

SETUP

One of the first signs of intelligence that Windows displays is during its installation process; accurately determining your PC's hardware configuration. However, you should always check the results.

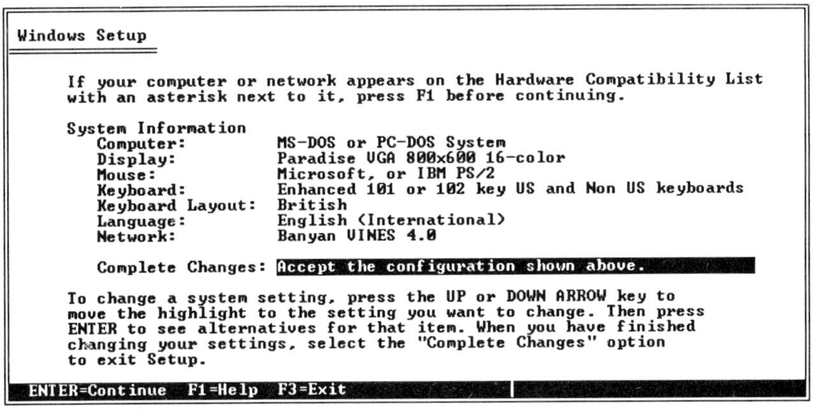

```
Windows Setup
───────────

     If your computer or network appears on the Hardware Compatibility List
     with an asterisk next to it, press F1 before continuing.

     System Information
        Computer:          MS-DOS or PC-DOS System
        Display:           Paradise UGA 800x600 16-color
        Mouse:             Microsoft, or IBM PS/2
        Keyboard:          Enhanced 101 or 102 key US and Non US keyboards
        Keyboard Layout:   British
        Language:          English (International)
        Network:           Banyan UINES 4.0

        Complete Changes:  Accept the configuration shown above.

     To change a system setting, press the UP or DOWN ARROW key to
     move the highlight to the setting you want to change. Then press
     ENTER to see alternatives for that item. When you have finished
     changing your settings, select the "Complete Changes" option
     to exit Setup.

 ENTER=Continue   F1=Help   F3=Exit
```

Figure 1.1 Windows SETUP program.

SETUP Parameters

The allowable parameters to SETUP are as follows:

SETUP /I   Disables hardware detection.

SETUP /P   Used to recreate Program Groups.

SETUP /N   Network installation switch, used to install Windows from a shared copy previously installed on a network server. Discussed at length later in this chapter.

However, just to make things confusing, some of these options cannot be specified when SETUP is run from a DOS prompt. Using these options incorrectly will either result in the error message 'Bad switch' being displayed or the SETUP screen will appear with an error message saying that the SETUP command cannot find the file SETUP.INF.

SETUP /I

If you have difficulty running SETUP on your machine, for example; the screen goes blank halfway through installation or SETUP stops inadvertently, you may have hardware that is incompatible with Windows' hardware detection mechanism.

To resolve this you can disable the hardware detection feature of the SETUP program by including an /I switch when you run it. For example:

```
SETUP /I
```

SETUP /P

An unfortunate feature of Windows is that program groups can become corrupted from time to time. The SETUP /P command can be used to recreate the standard PROGRAM MANAGER groups; Main, Accessories and Games.

The /P option should be thought of as a starting point for recreating your Windows environment. SETUP will not recreate any additional groups that you have created, neither will it insert any additional icons that you have added to the standard groups.

What SETUP Does Not Do

There are two things that SETUP does not do for the user. One is to set up a permanent swap file for use in 386 Enhanced mode. Running SWAPFILE, to set up a permanent swap file of contiguous disk space, increases Windows performance dramatically.

When running in 386 Enhanced mode Windows is able to utilise virtual memory to increase the number of applications that can run simultaneously. Virtual memory is a term used to describe a method where disk memory is used as RAM. By default Windows uses temporary swapfiles for virtual memory.

To be able to create a permanent swapfile you must have enough contiguous free disk space on your hard disk. An unfortunate side effect of the way MS-DOS stores files is that your disk becomes fragmented as it fills up, that is to say new files are not stored in contiguous space but may be broken into a number of small constituent parts distributed around the disk.

Windows suffers in two ways from file fragmentation. Firstly, performance of the drive is reduced significantly and secondly, on a badly fragmented drive there may not be enough contiguous space to create a permanent swapfile.

To cure file fragmentation you will need to purchase a disk reorganisation utility such as Speed Disk in Norton Utilities version 5 and 6. At the end of the day however you may find that your hard disk is full and no amount of reorganising and compacting will yield any additional space. In these circumstances the only option is to upgrade to a larger hard disk.

The method of creating a permanent swapfile is described in Chapter 7, Memory Management.

The final thing that SETUP could do is to put a WIN command line at the end of the AUTOEXEC.BAT file. We suggest that if you are using MS-DOS (as opposed to running Windows from within OS/2) you make Windows your primary working environment.

SYSEDIT

SYSEDIT is a System Configuration Editor supplied with Windows. It can be found in the SYSTEM sub-directory of your WINDOWS sub-directory. When run, it automatically edits the four most important files that deal with the configuration of a Windows session:

SYSTEM.INI
WIN.INI
CONFIG.SYS
AUTOEXEC.BAT

SYSEDIT provides the features that you would expect from an editor such as: cut, paste, and undo. The main benefit in using SYSEDIT is the ease with which you can amend or re-configure your system by running just one program.

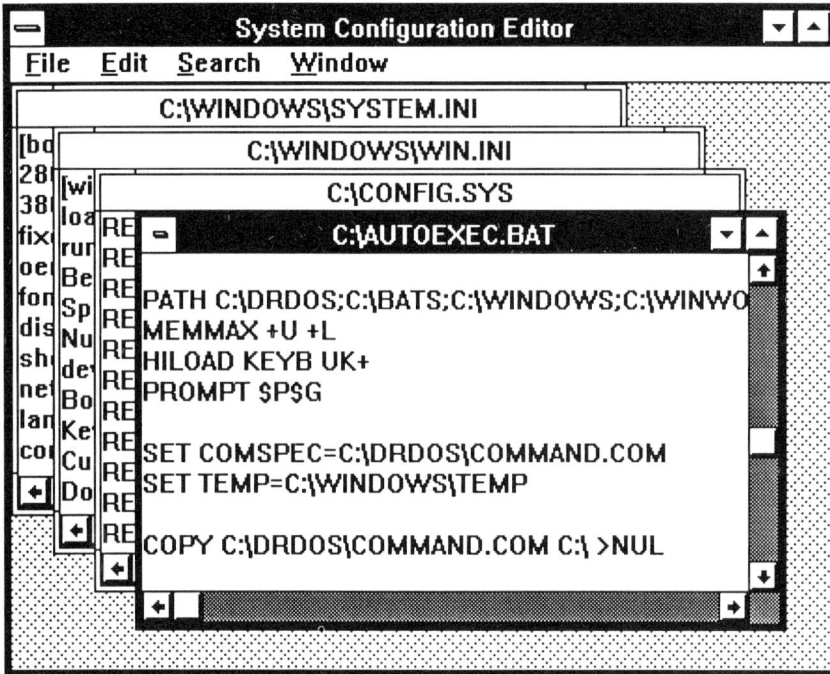

Figure 1.2 Windows SYSEDIT utility.

You can invoke SYSEDIT in one of two ways.

(1) In the PROGRAM MANAGER, pull down the FILE menu, select RUN and enter on the command line the following:

```
C:\WINDOWS\SYSTEM\SYSEDIT.EXE
```

Click on the OK button and then SYSEDIT will begin to execute.

(2) In the PROGRAM MANAGER, pull down the FILE menu and select the NEW option. Choose the PROGRAM ITEM option and enter the following in the PROGRAM ITEM PROPERTIES box:

```
C:\WINDOWS\SYSTEM\SYSEDIT.EXE
```

Enter a description such as 'System Editor' and then click on the OK button. The System Editor should then appear as an icon in your program group.

WIN.COM

Each time you install Windows (i.e. run SETUP), a file called WIN.COM is created. This is the program that runs when you type 'WIN' to load Windows. WIN.COM carries out several important tasks.

It finds out where Windows is located, checks for the existence of HIMEM.SYS (and/or any other Extended Memory Managers), loads PROGMAN.EXE, and finally displays Microsoft's standard logo screen.

SETUP, when it runs, combines three files to create WIN.COM. These are: a program loader WIN.CNF, a logo display routine (a .LGO file) and the start-up screen's graphics file (an .RLE file - Run-Length Encoded 4-bit).

The logo display routine is either called VGALOGO.LGO, EGALOGO.LGO, or whatever depending on the system configuration. Note that all these files are saved in the /SYSTEM subdirectory of your Windows directory. In the chapter 'Miscellaneous Hints and Tips' we describe how you can modify WIN.COM so that you can include your own individual startup screen such as a corporate logo.

SHARED COPIES OF WINDOWS ON NETWORKS

The last part of this chapter discusses: (i) A Network Administrator installing a shared copy of Windows onto a Local Area Network and (ii) a User installing Windows onto his PC from a shared copy installed (in (i) above) on a network.

If you are a Network Administrator we would encourage you to at least look at installing a shared copy of Windows onto a network server rather than on individual PCs as there are a number of benefits in doing so.

The very act of having to install Windows on a PC is a time consuming activity. As an individual user, inserting seven diskettes and replying to a few prompts is not too bad, but take the case of a small business with, say, ten PCs, or a large corporation with thousands - then, installation, maintenance and upgrading of all this software starts to become a major headache. Someone has to support all that software and with each PC probably being configured slightly different from the next, the problems for technical support groups have just started.

It says a lot for the flexibility of Windows that this shared copy approach works and as we will soon see, System or Network Administrators can easily tailor the network-installed Windows system in order to make their networked Windows users life a lot simpler.

INSTALLING WINDOWS ON A NETWORK

This procedure is outlined in the Windows User's Guide but is documented here for completeness. Before you start you will need to create the batch file shown in figure 1.3.

```
A:
FOR %%I IN (*.*) DO W:\WINDOWS\EXPAND %%I W:\WINDOWS\%%I
W:
```

Figure 1.3 EXPALL.BAT for installing Windows on a network.

Then assuming that, as a network administrator, you are copying Windows from the supplied Windows installation diskettes in drive A: to a \WINDOWS network directory on a network disk drive, say, W:, you will need to follow the instructions shown below.

(1) Copy the EXPAND.EXE program from Windows Disk #2 onto a network drive (in our example W:\WINDOWS).

(2) Insert Windows Disk #1 (into drive A:) and invoke the batch file EXPALL:

```
EXPALL A:\*.* W:\WINDOWS
```

(3) Repeat for the remaining Windows disks.

Everything Windows needs, and a user needs, for running SETUP is now present in that network drive and directory.

SETUP /N

SETUP with a /N (network) switch is designed to be used by users of PCs attached to a local area network where a shared copy of Windows has been previously installed on a network server.

Using SETUP is simple. Users should connect to the network (in the usual manner), change to the directory where Windows is located on the network (in the previous examples this has been W:\WINDOWS), type SETUP /N and then follow the instructions on the screen.

SETUP copies some Windows files to a user's personal Windows directory (usually located on a hard disk). By maintaining individual copies of these files users can customise Windows according to their own preferences even though they are sharing most Windows files with other users on the network.

SETUP.INF

The Windows SETUP program uses this file, among other reasons, to determine the initial contents of the user's PROGRAM MANAGER groups, to specify what files should be locally copied to the users' Windows directory, to specify what should be removed from a user's CONFIG.SYS file and to make additions to files such as WIN.INI.

System or Network Administrators can edit the file SETUP.INF (found in the Windows /SYSTEM directory) to help users correctly install Windows from a network (i.e. to set the correct default settings), to add or remove applications in the PROGRAM MANAGER groups and to customise other settings.

If you are a network administrator and have already installed a shared copy of Windows on the network or are considering doing so we strongly suggest that you familiarise yourself with the settings in the SETUP.INF file.

Let's look in some detail at the sorts of things that network administrators can and should tailor.

Remember, be very careful when amending SETUP.INF and always make a back-up before doing any changes.

README.TXT

You may wish your network users to read specific information or notes from yourself or your organisation after they have run SETUP /N and installed a shared copy of Windows. This can be done by finding and amending the setting shown in figure 1.4. Replace the README.TXT with your own Notepad file.

```
[data]
; this is the cmd line that is executed for the online docs
readme = "notepad /.setup readme.txt"
```

Figure 1.4 SETUP.INF settings for README.TXT.

Alternatively you can just amend README.TXT file and add your own information as required.

Language

The default language and keyboard country codes are US. If you are not in the US you may wish to change them to reflect your country codes. To do this, find both the deflang and defkeydll settings as shown in figure 1.5.

```
[data]
deflang = usa
; this indicates what country you are in via the country keyboard
; DLL.  we special case the usadll to see if we are in the USA
defkeydll = usadll
```

Figure 1.5 The SETUP.INF setting for the Welcome message.

To change from US to a particular language you need to find the correct three character abbreviation for that language. You can do this by looking at the [keyboard.tables] setting, also found in SETUP.INF. This is shown in figure 1.6.

```
[keyboard.tables]
beldll = 2:kbdbe.dll , "Belgian"
```

```
candll = 2:kbdca.dll , "French Canadian"
dandll = 2:kbdda.dll , "Danish"
fredll = 2:kbdfr.dll , "French"
findll = 2:kbdfi.dll , "Finnish"
gerdll = 2:kbdgr.dll , "German"
icedll = 2:kbdic.dll , "Icelandic"
itadll = 2:kbdit.dll , "Italian"
latdll = 2:kbdla.dll , "Latin American"
dutdll = 2:kbdne.dll , "Dutch"
nordll = 2:kbdno.dll , "Norwegian"
pordll = 2:kbdpo.dll , "Portuguese"
swedll = 2:kbdsw.dll , "Swedish"
swfdll = 2:kbdsf.dll , "Swiss French"
swgdll = 2:kbdsg.dll , "Swiss German"
spadll = 2:kbdsp.dll , "Spanish"
bridll = 2:kbduk.dll , "British"
usadll = 2:kbdus.dll , "US"
usddll = 2:kbddv.dll , "US-Dvorak"
usxdll = 2:kbdusx.dll, "US-International"
```

Figure 1.6 The SETUP.INF keyboard tables.

So, for example, to default your users' installation from US to British you would set deflang and defkeydll to BRI and BRIDLL respectively.

Bitmaps

Some settings found in SETUP.INF control what Windows actually copies to a user's hard disk (or in the case of diskless workstations to a networked drive as we will see later) during installation. You may wish to amend some of these entries, either to save disk space or because you do not want users to have access to those particular files or applications (a good example might be the games!).

```
[win.bmps]
     5:PYRAMID.BMP,        "Background bitmaps"
     5:CHESS.BMP
     5:WEAVE.BMP
     5:BOXES.BMP
     5:PAPER.BMP
     5:PARTY.BMP
     5:RIBBONS.BMP
```

Figure 1.7 Default bitmap files.

Bitmaps are generally large files and can take up a lot of disk space. It is easy to either have some of them not copied or to replace some of them with your own standard or corporate bitmaps. The [win.bmps] entry, shown in figure 1.7, is the entry that needs to be changed. Either remove lines or amend entries to reflect the changes you require.

Text Files

The same thing that applies to bitmaps also applies to TXT files. Most network users will not wish to read the sort of detailed information that is found in the standard Windows TXT files. The [win.readme] setting, shown in figure 1.8, controls what is copied across. Lines can simply be removed as necessary.

```
[win.readme]
    5:readme.txt,          "Readme files"
    5:networks.txt
    5:printers.txt
    5:winini.txt
    5:winini2.txt
    5:sysini.txt
    5:sysini2.txt
    5:sysini3.txt
    5:3270.txt
```

Figure 1.8 Windows online text files.

Applications

If there are applications that you do not wish your users to use or to be copied onto their local hard drives then you can remove their entries from the [win.apps] setting, shown in figure 1.9. You should also remove any entries in the [progman.groups] section, discussed in the next section, so that Windows does not try to set up the (non-existent) applications, together with their icons, in a group window.

```
[win.apps]
    3:PROGMAN.EXE,          "Windows Program Manager"
    4:TASKMAN.EXE,          "Windows Task Manager"
    3:WINFILE.EXE,          "Windows File Manager"
    3:CALC.EXE,             "Windows Calculator"
    3:CALENDAR.EXE,         "Windows Calendar"
    3:CARDFILE.EXE,         "Windows Cardfile"
    4:CLIPBRD.EXE,          "Windows Clipboard"
    4:CLOCK.EXE,            "Windows Clock"
    3:DIGITAL.FON,          "Windows Clock"
    3:CONTROL.EXE,          "Windows Control Panel"
    3:NOTEPAD.EXE,          "Windows Notepad"
    3:PBRUSH.EXE,           "Windows Paintbrush"
    3:PBRUSH.DLL,           "Windows Paintbrush"
    3:PIFEDIT.EXE,          "Windows PIF Editor"
    3:RECORDER.EXE,         "Windows Macro Recorder"
    3:RECORDER.DLL,         "Windows Macro Recorder"
    4:REVERSI.EXE,          "Windows Reversi"
    3:PRINTMAN.EXE,         "Windows Print Manager"
    3:SOL.EXE,              "Windows Solitaire"
    4:TERMINAL.EXE,         "Windows Terminal"
    3:WRITE.EXE,            "Windows Write"
    3:MSDOS.EXE,            "MS-DOS Executive"
```

Figure 1.9 Windows application programs.

For any applications that you have removed it is obviously sensible to remove any associated help files.

```
[win.help]
    4:CALC.HLP,             "Windows Calculator help"
    4:CALENDAR.HLP,         "Windows Calendar help"
    5:CARDFILE.HLP,         "Windows Cardfile help"
    4:CLIPBRD.HLP,          "Windows Clipboard help"
    4:CONTROL.HLP,          "Windows Control Panel help"
    4:NOTEPAD.HLP,          "Windows Notepad help"
    4:PBRUSH.HLP,           "Windows Paintbrush help"
    4:PIFEDIT.HLP,          "Windows PIF Editor help"
    4:PRINTMAN.HLP,         "Windows Print Manager help"
    4:PROGMAN.HLP,          "Windows Program Manager help"
    4:RECORDER.HLP,         "Windows Recorder help"
    5:REVERSI.HLP,          "Windows Reversi help"
    4:SOL.HLP,              "Windows Solitaire help"
    4:TERMINAL.HLP,         "Windows Terminal help"
    4:WINFILE.HLP,          "Windows File Manager help"
    4:WRITE.HLP,            "Windows Write help"
```

Figure 1.10 Windows application help files.

This can be done by deleting entries in the [win.help] section, shown in figure 1.10.

Program Groups

Windows sets up groups according to the entries found in the [progman.groups] setting. Entries for the three standard Windows 3.0 default groups are shown in figure 1.11.

```
[progman.groups]
Main,1
Accessories
Games
```

Figure 1.11 The program group entries in the SETUP.INF file.

Immediately following the [progman.groups] setting you will see more settings, one for each of the groups you specified in the [progman.groups]. The three sections and their entries for the three standard default groups are shown in figure 1.12 (alteration of these values will also affect the way SETUP /P works).

```
[Main]
"File Manager",          WINFILE.EXE
"Control Panel",         CONTROL.EXE
"Print Manager",         PRINTMAN.EXE
"Clipboard",             CLIPBRD.EXE
"DOS Prompt",            COMMAND.COM, PROGMAN.EXE, 1
"Windows Setup",         SETUP.EXE

[Accessories]
"Write",                 WRITE.EXE
"Paintbrush",            PBRUSH.EXE
"Terminal",              TERMINAL.EXE
"Notepad",               NOTEPAD.EXE
"Calendar",              CALENDAR.EXE
"Calculator",            CALC.EXE
"Clock",                 CLOCK.EXE
"PIF Editor",            PIFEDIT.EXE
[Games]
"Solitaire",             SOL.EXE
"Reversi",               REVERSI.EXE
```

Figure 1.12 Program entries for each PROGRAM MANAGER group.

If you have removed applications from being copied onto the user's hard disk then you need to amend or delete the appropriate entries found in figure 1.12. If you wish to remove groups then delete the appropriate entries from the [progman.groups] setting and also the group setting name following it.

To add new groups, add a new line to the [progman.groups] section and then build a new group with that name with all the applications you wish to have entered in it. The example in figure 1.13 adds a new group called Finance.

```
[progman.groups]
Main,1
Accessories
Finance

[Finance]
"Write",                WRITE.EXE
"Excel",                EXCEL.EXE
"Sales System",         3270.COM
```

Figure 1.13 Adding program groups to the SETUP.INF file.

WIN.INI

A special section called [wininiupdate] allows items to be added automatically to the user's WIN.INI file during SETUP and installation. The only difficulty in using this setting is knowing the correct format for entries. Figure 1.14 shows an example of a setting found by default in the SETUP.INF file.

```
[wininiupdate]
extensions,pcx,"pbrush.exe ^.pcx"
```

Figure 1.14 Adding an entry to the [Extensions] section in WIN.INI.

To get an idea of the format, let's compare what is shown in figure 1.14, with what we actually get in the WIN.INI file...

```
[Extensions]
pcx=pbrush.exe ^.pcx
```

Comparing the two, we can see that the first item in [wininiupdate] is the section name in WIN.INI, the second item is the entry (followed by an equals sign) and the third item is the application name and associated extension. Each item is separated by a comma. You may wish to help your users by automatically adding extensions for applications that they are likely to use, for example something like Microsoft Visual Basic or Microsoft Excel.

Following the conventions we have just discovered, it is now a simple matter to add other entries. For example, if we wanted to add LOAD= or RUN= entries to force certain applications to run automatically when our users run Windows we could do so by adding an entry to [wininiupdate] like that shown in figure 1.15.

```
[wininiupdate]
windows,load,"phone.exe"
```

Figure 1.15 Adding a LOAD entry to the [Windows] section in WIN.INI.

If PHONE.EXE were an in-house written application we might like it to be automatically loaded and run as an icon on each user's workstation by default. The example in figure 1.15 would configure a user's WIN.INI to do exactly that.

DISKLESS WORKSTATIONS

Installing Windows on to a diskless workstation (i.e. a machine without a hard disk) connected to a network where a shared copy of Windows has previously been installed is a simple enough task. If some or all of your users haven't got a hard disk then you will need to tell them to indicate to SETUP on which network drive they can place their local Windows files. There is a 'defdir' setting in the

SETUP.INF file which indicates the name and locations of the default windows directory (i.e. C:\WINDOWS).

We believe that as more organisations move towards high powered PC networks and standardise on graphical user interfaces, such as Windows, diskless workstations will come into their own due to their relative simplicity, their ease of use, the simplified task of maintenance and support and the fact that there is no threat to the network from viruses.

You will probably see many more PCs built and marketed solely for the Diskless Workstation arena. These will probably be based on Intel486 CPU technology and come complete with high-resolution graphics, large display monitors, a mouse and built in high-speed Ethernet adaptor. Everything you want in fact for a good, easy to use and most of all safe, network client.

PRE-INSTALL

Microsoft have been working closely with many Original Equipment Manufacturers (OEMs) and we will soon start to see more PCs come to market already installed with both MS-DOS 5.0 and Windows version 3.x.

In actual fact, the idea of pre-installing Windows onto a box is the next logical step in ease of use and will make PCs much more accessible. All the user needs to do is plug in a monitor, keyboard and mouse, start the PC up and then rather than being presented with the unfriendly C: prompt, they see the Windows desktop.

CHAPTER

2

OPERATING MODES

Windows 3.0 is accessed by running WIN.COM and depending on your machine configuration can be run in one of three modes, Real, Standard or 386 Enhanced. Windows 3.1 is the same except there is no support for Real mode. If you do not choose a mode, Windows picks the one most suitable to your hardware.

On Intel 8088/8086 microprocessor based machines (only possible with Windows 3.0), Real mode is selected. Standard mode is selected on machines with an 80286 microprocessor and at least 192K of extended memory free. Standard mode is also selected on machines with Intel386 or Intel486 microprocessors that have less than 1024K extended memory free.

386 Enhanced mode offers the user the most power and flexibility and operates on any Intel386 or Intel486 microprocessor-based PCs that have 1024K of extended memory free.

It is possible to force Windows into a specific mode from the command line. For example Real mode (only available with Windows 3.0) is selected by typing:

```
WIN /R
```

Standard mode (machines with 80286 or later processors) by typing:

```
WIN /S
```

386 Enhanced mode (machines with an Intel386 microprocessor or later) by typing:

```
WIN /3
```

WINDOWS STARTUP PARAMETERS

In addition to the parameters specifying the operating mode, you can also supply as a parameter the name of a program that you wish to be started up when you first get into Windows. For example:

```
WIN CLOCK
WIN C:\WINDOWS\CLOCK
```

will both start up Windows and the Windows CLOCK. If you wanted the CLOCK to run but needed to start up Windows in Standard mode, then you would type:

```
WIN /S CLOCK
```

One benefit of supplying a further parameter to the WIN command (not /R, /S or /3) is that you will not be shown the Microsoft Windows copyright screen during loading.

MODE DETERMINATION

After first installing Windows or after doing any form of system configuration (whether it be something as simple as amending CONFIG.SYS to increase the size of your disk cache or a hardware addition such as adding a new network card) you should always check the mode that Windows is running in to make sure that this matches your expectations.

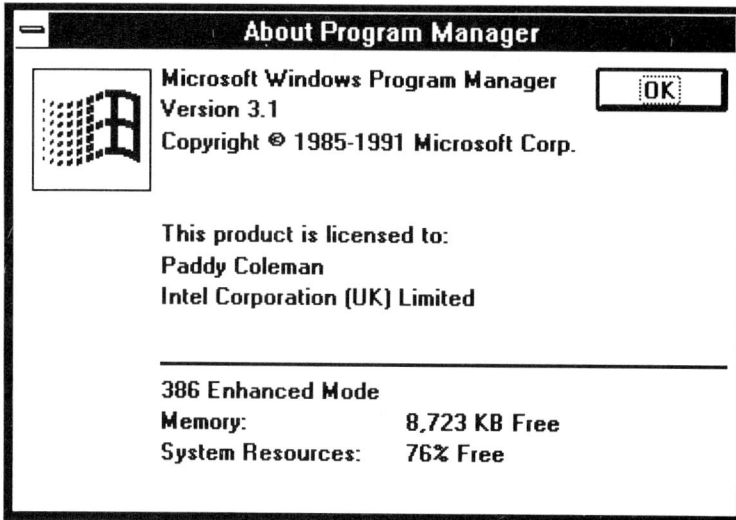

Figure 2.1 Windows 3.1 About Program Manager dialog box.

To determine the mode that Windows is currently running in, pull-down the HELP menu in the PROGRAM MANAGER and select the ABOUT PROGRAM MANAGER option. The dialog box in figure 2.1 will be displayed. As can be seen the information presented includes the Windows version number (3.1 in this case), the mode and the amount of free memory.

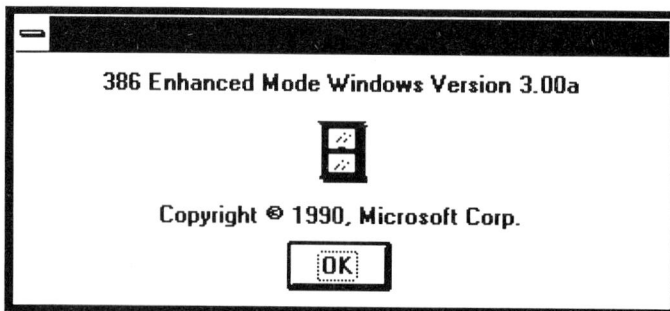

Figure 2.2 WINVER dialog box.

To display the Windows version number on its own either type WINVER at the DOS prompt, or execute WINVER from the RUN option in the PROGRAM MANAGER FILE menu. The latter will display the dialog box in figure 2.2.

STANDARD MODE

A little publicised feature of MS-DOS 5.0 is that if you are using it in conjunction with Windows and are taking advantage of the upper memory blocks (i.e. UMBs) you will be unable to run Windows in Standard Mode. Note that in order to take advantage of the UMBs you would typically install EMM386.EXE, specify DOS=HIGH,UMB in your CONFIG.SYS file and be using a machine with an Intel386 or Intel486 microprocessor.

If you specifically request Standard mode (by entering WIN /S) you will receive an error message "Cannot run Windows in Standard mode; check to ensure you are not running other protected-mode software, or run in Real mode", otherwise you will be placed in Real mode by default.

To get around this you will have to disable EMM386 and not take advantage of some of the high memory support that MS-DOS 5.0 offers.

Looking at the technicalities of the memory management software involved (i.e. EMM386) this was to be expected. For example, Qualitas who have had their very sophisticated and powerful 386MAX memory management software on the market for some time now, only support Windows 3.0 in Real or 386 Enhanced mode.

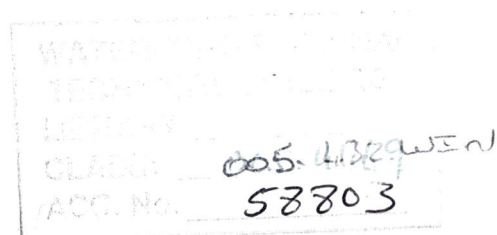

NO ENHANCED MODE?

Even if you have the system requirements necessary for Windows to boot up in 386 Enhanced mode, there are a few reasons why it may not do so.

CONFIG.SYS FILES ENTRY

Windows will not load in 386 Enhanced mode unless your CONFIG.SYS file contains a FILES statement.

You may find that Windows works correctly in Real or Standard mode, but will either hang at the title screen, or return you to the DOS command prompt when you try to start up in 386 Enhanced mode. Adding (or increasing to) a FILES=30 line to your CONFIG.SYS file will correct this problem.

MS-DOS 5.0 AND WINA20.386

If you are using MS-DOS 5.0 you will be unable to run Windows in 386 Enhanced mode unless MS-DOS or Windows can find and load the file WINA20.386. This is fully detailed in Chapter 6, MS-DOS 5.0.

WindowMemSize

A useful SYSTEM.INI entry is the setting WindowMemSize. This limits the amount of conventional memory that Windows can use for itself, the default value being -1 which indicates to Windows that it can use as much of this memory as it needs.

If you do not have quite enough memory to run Windows in 386 Enhanced mode you can try entering a positive value less than 640 to see if you can get your machine to go into 386 Enhanced mode.

BENEFITS OF 386 ENHANCED MODE

Some Windows users, who do not run native MS-DOS applications, advocate running their systems in Standard mode, even though they have the full system requirements needed to run in 386 Enhanced mode. The justification for selecting Standard over 386 Enhanced mode is the 10-15% performance increase. Not running native MS-DOS applications means that they have no requirement to either multi-task MS-DOS applications or run MS-DOS applications in a window.

What they lose of course is the virtual memory support (i.e. swapfile - discussed in a later chapter) which can dramatically increase performance of a system but only works in 386 Enhanced mode.

We suggest that you always use 386 Enhanced mode as it is the most powerful and flexible of all the modes. If you do not have a machine capable of running in this mode then it might be possible to upgrade it!

REJUVENATING YOUR 80286 BASED PC

Individuals, small businesses and large organisations may have some older 80286 microprocessor-based PCs. Often, these can be easily and affordably upgraded so that they can run Windows in 386 Enhanced mode. There are various upgrade products currently on the market. Three of them are listed below and are then discussed in more detail:

(1) Intel SnapIn 386 Module.

(2) AOX MicroMaster.

(3) Kingston Technology SX/NOW.

More importantly the upgrades will be necessary if you wish to run the more powerful 32-bit version of Windows that Microsoft plans to release. The new versions of Windows and 32-bit software in particular are discussed in the final chapter of this book.

Intel SnapIn 386

In May 1991 Intel announced SnapIn 386, a compact upgrade module that increases the capability of an IBM 80286 based PS/2 to that of an Intel386SX microprocessor-based machine (running at 20Mhz). Street prices at present are approximately $360-400 USD.

The SnapIn 386 module plugs directly into the CPU socket of an IBM PS/2 Model 50, Model 50Z or Model 60. To install a SnapIn 386 module, one simply uses the chip puller provided to remove the PS/2's original 80286 chip from its socket and then plugs in the replacement module. There are no cables, jumpers or switches on the module and installation typically takes approximately 15 minutes.

The SnapIn 386 module's design includes 16K of memory cache (which boosts system performance) and is supplied with device drivers for both MS-DOS and OS/2.

SnapIn 386 currently only works in IBM PS/2 models 50 or 60 although there are plans to release SnapIn modules for other popular 80286 based Personal Computers.

AOX MicroMaster

AOX Incorporated is a pioneer in engineering both PC and PS/2 board level products which enhance microcomputer functionality and speed. The AOX MicroMaster is a processor on a card that can take over the main CPU from your existing IBM PS/2 processor. This is possible due to the bus-mastering feature of IBM's powerful Micro Channel Architecture (MCA).

If you have an IBM PS/2 model 50 or 60 an AOX card will give you the 32-bit power of an Intel386 microprocessor. It is also possible to upgrade any PS/2, model 50 or above (whether it be 80286 or Intel386 CPU based) to an Intel486 microprocessor using the AOX 486-25 card.

The available AOX MicroMaster products to date are:

    AOX 386-20. An Intel386 DX running at 20Mhz.
    AOX 386-25. An Intel386 DX running at 25Mhz.
    AOX 386-33. An Intel386 DX running at 33Mhz.
    AOX 486-25. An Intel486 DX running at 25Mhz.

Each AOX MicroMaster 386 adaptor has a socket to allow the addition of an Intel387 Math Co-processor and each card can be configured to hold up to 8MB memory using IBM 1, 2 or 4MB SIMMs (Single In-line Memory Modules).

The card takes up one 16-bit micro-channel slot inside the PS/2 and can be installed relatively easily, although we found that with other cards already installed in the PS/2 the configuration via the IBM Reference Diskette took a little time to get correct.

AOX MicroMaster products are relatively expensive, the cheapest being approximately $1000 USD.

Kingston Technology SX/NOW

Kingston Technology is a Californian add-on memory manufacturer and is the supplier of a processor upgrade product called SX/NOW.

The SX/NOW plugs directly into an Intel 80286 microprocessor slot on an IBM PS/2 Model 50, Model 50Z or Model 60's system board and upgrades the PC to either a 16Mhz or 20Mhz Intel386 SX microprocessor. SX/NOW also contains a 16kb memory cache for additional performance and a co-processor socket for a genuine Intel387 Math Co-Processor.

Upgrades may soon be available for other popular 80286 based personal computers, with Compaq and AST probably being the next machines to have the SX/NOW option available. The 16Mhz and 20Mhz versions are, respectively, approximately $700 and $800 each.

MULTI-TASKING

Whilst we are on the subject of operating modes it is probably a convenient place to talk about how Windows multi-tasks. People often get confused about multi-tasking and tie themselves in knots pondering the differences and meanings of terms like pre-emptive, non pre-emptive and time-slicing.

Simply remember this. Multi-tasking is the ability of a single microprocessor based system to give the appearance of executing several programs or applications simultaneously. The current multi-tasking features of Windows are what we call non pre-emptive multi-tasking.

Pre-emptive multi-tasking operating systems (such as OS/2) make use of a time-sliced priority based scheduler that allows the operating system to directly slice microprocessor time between all its currently executing tasks. What this means is that an executing OS/2 application does not surrender CPU time whenever it wishes - the OS/2 scheduler pre-empts it, basically wrestling away control from the application whenever the operating system wishes.

The reason that Windows has historically been a non pre-emptive multi-tasking environment is due to the Real mode memory limitations on which Windows was originally based.

There is nothing essentially wrong with non pre-emptive multi-tasking provided that Windows applications are developed in such a way that they frequently return control to the operating system - that is, they do not hog the processor!

Forthcoming versions of Windows will run all applications pre-emptively. This will allow smoother task switching and better background operation.

THE DEATH OF REAL MODE

Real mode, because it is based around very old Intel 8086/8088 microprocessor technology is not supported in Windows version 3.1. The reason for this is simple enough; as the functionality of Windows increases and developers take advantage of this, their applications become more sophisticated. The 1MB memory limitation of Real mode and the constraints this causes on the underlying Windows Real mode are simply not powerful enough to handle this level of sophistication.

'NT' MODE

NT stands for New Technology and is the name given by Microsoft to a completely new operating system kernel that they have developed. It has been designed to be the basis for a scalable, portable and industrial strength operating system, which has been named Windows NT.

The NT kernel will be scalable because it will run on a range of differing power platforms, from notebook and laptop PCs, to desktop and deskside workstations right up to file, network and database servers and superservers.

The portability comes about because the kernel is designed to run the same, whether it be on the industry standard Intel microprocessor architecture or on other microprocessor architectures that Microsoft decide to 'port' the kernel to.

An industrial strength operating system must first of all be secure. The NT kernel meets what is classed as the C2 security classification.

It also needs to take advantage of something that is becoming more and more popular with PC manufacturers today and that is Multi-Processing - i.e. having more than one microprocessor in the PC to share the workload. The NT kernel does this by having in-built Symmetrical Multi-Processing (SMP) support.

WINDOWS NT

By using the NT kernel as the basis for Windows, as opposed to MS-DOS, Windows can develop from the operating environment it is now to a fully-fledged operating system.

Microsoft often describe NT as the third Windows mode, the other two being Standard and 386 Enhanced mode (now that Real mode has gone) which can be rather confusing.

In summary then, Windows NT, mainly because of the new NT kernel, will provide pre-emptive multi-tasking, be more fault tolerant, will provide symmetrical multi-processor support and will be truly 32-bit - the latter offering much superior performance than any current Windows versions.

CHAPTER

3

INITIALISATION FILES

Windows and its applications make extensive use of initialisation files (files that end with an INI extension). When installed, Windows creates the following in the WINDOWS sub-directory:

CONTROL.INI
PROGMAN.INI
SYSTEM.INI
WIN.INI
WINFILE.INI

This chapter deals specifically with the Windows initialisation files that can be edited to allow configuration of your Windows environment. Namely the SYSTEM and WIN initialisation files.

CONTROL, PROGMAN and WINFILE are used by the Windows CONTROL PANEL, PROGRAM MANAGER and FILE MANAGER respectively and should not normally be edited manually. These are dealt with in more detail in the Windows Applications chapter of this book.

Windows initialisation files generally follow a common format. Almost always they are broken up into logical sections. and each section contains a number of different settings. This format is shown in figure 3.1.

```
[section name]
keyname=value
```

Figure 3.1 Common format of Windows initialisation files

In figure 3.1, [section name] is the name of a section. Sections, as we already mentioned, are used to break settings into logical groups. The enclosing brackets ([ ]) are required, and the left bracket must be in the leftmost column on the screen.

The keyname=value statement defines the value of each setting. A keyname is the name of a setting. It can consist of any combination of letters and digits, and must be followed immediately by an equal sign (=). The value of the setting can be an integer, a Boolean value, a string, or a quoted string, depending on the setting. There are multiple settings in most sections.

Comments can be included in initialisation files, but each line of comments must begin with a semi-colon (;) in column 1.

The Windows CONTROL PANEL is the normal way to introduce changes into your Windows configuration (this modifies and adds settings to both WIN and SYSTEM.INI). However, many of the settings in these two INI files cannot be changed through the Windows CONTROL PANEL and so you will have to edit the file manually to make modifications.

N.B.   Always take a backup of an INI file before you edit it!

You should take great care whenever making changes in this way. Incorrect changes to INI files can lead to unexpected results when you run Windows or may disable your system. Some text editors can damage certain characters (those with ASCII values of greater than 127). It is recommended that you use NOTEPAD or SYSEDIT as a text editor.

SYSTEM.INI

SYSTEM.INI primarily contains settings that allow you to customise Windows to match your system's hardware. It contains global system information that Windows uses when it starts. Any changes to the file do not take effect until you restart Windows.

The following sections can appear in the SYSTEM.INI file:

SECTION	PURPOSE
[boot]	Lists drivers and Windows modules.
[boot.description]	Lists the names of devices you can change using Windows SETUP
[keyboard]	Contains information about the keyboard.
[NonWindowsApp]	Contains information used by non-Windows applications.
[standard]	Contains information used by Windows in Standard mode.
[386Enh]	Contains information used by Windows in 386 Enhanced mode.

When changing settings in the SYSTEM.INI file, you need to be very careful; changing a setting incorrectly may disable your system.

WIN.INI

The settings in the WIN.INI file allow you to personalise your Windows environment. WIN.INI contains several sections, each of which consists of a group of related settings. Your WIN.INI file might not have all of these sections or it might have additional ones, depending on your system's hardware and software configuration.

The following sections can appear in WIN.INI:

SECTION	PURPOSE
[windows]	Affects an assortment of elements in your Windows environment.
[desktop]	Controls the appearance of the screen background (desktop) and the positioning of icons.
[extensions]	Associates specified types of files with corresponding applications.
[intl]	Describes how to display items for countries other than the US.
[ports]	Lists all available output ports.
[fonts]	This describes the screen font files that are loaded by Windows.
[PrinterPorts]	Lists active and inactive output devices.
[devices]	Lists active output devices that provide compatibility with Windows 2.x applications.
[colors]	Defines colours for parts of the Windows display.

When changing settings in the WIN.INI file, you need to be very careful; changing a setting incorrectly may lead to unexpected results.

'Other' Sections in the WIN.INI File

When you install Windows applications you may find that they insert text into the WIN.INI file. This will normally consist of a section heading naming the application, followed by a group of related settings. These settings should be fully explained in the application's documentation; you may also find explanations in the Windows Applications chapter of this document.

```
[Clock]
iFormat=0

[Solitaire]
Back=11
Options=9

[Freemem]
Position=544,6
```

Figure 3.2 Applications as sections in the WIN.INI file.

As you can see in figure 3.2, each setting is of importance to the application. In [Solitaire] for example, the back of the playing cards is set. An Options setting relates to the OPTION pull down menu within SOLITAIRE.

[Freemem] is a utility that displays the amount of free memory available when Windows is running. Its setting here in WIN.INI (Position=544,6) gives the position on the screen where its window is first displayed.

WIN.INI [Windows] Section

LOAD and RUN are two settings found in the [Windows] section of the WIN.INI file. They instruct Windows to run or load specific applications when Windows is started. The format of the settings are as follows:

```
RUN=filename(s)
LOAD=filename(s)
```

where FILENAME(S) is a list of one or more filenames of applications, or documents associated with applications (made via the [extensions] section - see later), each separated by a space.

RUN tells Windows to run the appropriate application when Windows is started and LOAD specifies one or more applications that are to be run as icons when Windows is started.

```
[windows]
LOAD=CLOCK.EXE WINFILE.EXE
RUN=WIN.INI
```

Figure 3.3 Example LOAD and RUN settings.

The examples in figure 3.3 would start up the Windows CLOCK and run it as an icon (at the bottom of your screen), start up the FILE MANAGER application as an icon and also edit the file WIN.INI (using the NOTEPAD because of the association between the INI extension and the NOTEPAD application made in the [extensions] section of the WIN.INI file).

If you follow our suggestions in Appendix C about creating sub-directories to hold games, utilities, etc. and you have a utility you wish to run from WIN.INI (i.e. something not in the WINDOWS sub-directory), you can execute it with the following setting:

```
[windows]
LOAD=C:\WINDOWS\UTILS\your-utility
```

where YOUR-UTILITY is the name of the application you wish to run.

WIN.INI [Extension] Section

This section contains settings that link groups of document files with an application. This means that when you open one of the document files, the appropriate application will start automatically.

```
[Extensions]
cal=calendar.exe ^.cal
crd=cardfile.exe ^.crd
trm=terminal.exe ^.trm
txt=NOTEPAD.exe ^.txt
ini=NOTEPAD.exe ^.ini
pcx=pbrush.exe ^.pcx
bmp=pbrush.exe ^.bmp
wri=write.exe ^.wri
rec=recorder.exe ^.rec
```

Figure 3.4 Example [Extensions] section in the WIN.INI file.

The format of the entries in figure 3.4 is EXTENSION=COMMAND-LINE. The EXTENSION keyname is a filename extension of one to three characters. The COMMAND-LINE always begins with an application filename (with the EXE extension). This can be followed by any command parameters the application needs, usually including the document filename. The caret (^) character can be used when the original document filename is needed in the command line; the caret is replaced by the document filename without any extension.

The most typical EXTENSION entries simply list the application name and the document name.

    CAL=CALENDAR.EXE ^.CAL

If you access a file called MYFILE.CAL after this association has been made, the CALENDAR program will start and automatically open the file named MYFILE. These settings should be changed by selecting CHOOSE ASSOCIATE from the FILE menu in the FILE MANAGER and not by editing the WIN.INI file.

WIN.INI [Colours] Section

Many people find that the predefined Windows colour schemes are too bright, have too many contrasts and are hard on the eyes for daily use. This is partly due to the high intensity white window backgrounds which are much brighter than those found in typical DOS applications.

Looking through CONTROL PANEL's predefined colour schemes it is hard to find any that are easier on the eyes as they all use the same bright white window background.

There are many system colours (including the highlight selection text and background colours) that CONTROL PANEL does not let you set. However, you can do this by editing the WIN.INI file. Figure 3.5 is an example of a colour scheme that you can try by typing the following into your WIN.INI. It is designed to be a low contrast scheme.

```
[colors]
;
; CONTROL PANEL knows about these and you will find
; them all in your standard (unamended) WIN.INI.
```

```
;
; We have however placed them in alphabetical order!
;
ActiveBorder=                    128  255  255
ActiveTitle=                       0  128   64
AppWorkspace=                     64  128  128
Background=                      128  128  128
InactiveBorder=                 192  192  192
InactiveTitle=              128  128  128
Menu=                              0  128  128
MenuText=                          0    0    0
Scrollbar=                       191  191  191
TitleText=                       255  255  255
Window=                          192  192  192
WindowFrame=                       0    0    0
WindowText=                        0    0    0
;
; CONTROL PANEL does not know anything about the
; following ...
;
;ButtonFace=
;ButtonShadow=
ButtonText=                        0    0    0
GreyText=                        128  128  128
Hilight=                         128    0    0
HilightText=                     255  255    0
```

Figure 3.5 [colors] section of the WIN.INI file.

Since many Windows controls are painted with pairs of fixed Bit-maps representing the pushed and un-pushed states, playing with the values of the ButtonFace and ButtonShadow settings has no affect on most 3-dimensional controls.   Therefore, even though they exist (although CONTROL PANEL does not know about them) we have not assigned any value to them in figure 3.5.

MORE DETAIL ON INDIVIDUAL SETTINGS

Microsoft supply detailed information on almost all the settings found in the files WIN.INI and SYSTEM.INI if only you know where to look. The on-line files shown below can normally be found in your Windows sub-directory and cover most settings:

WININI.TXT
WININ2.TXT
SYSINI.TXT
SYSINI2.TXT
SYSINI3.TXT

OTHER INITIALISATION FILES

Any Windows application is free to write information to the WIN.INI file. However Microsoft encourage software developers to have their applications write to their own dedicated INI files (so that the size of the WIN.INI file can be kept to a minimum).

Therefore as you install Windows software applications other initialisation files will probably be created. For example the Adobe Type Manager utility creates a file called ATM.INI, Microsoft Visual Basic creates a file called VB.INI, Microsoft Excel creates EXCEL.INI and Microsoft Word for Windows creates WINWORD.INI (although WINWORD also writes to WIN.INI!).

Normally these are all valid Notepad text files. They can be opened, browsed and edited if necessary in the normal Notepad manner.

However, you will occasionally come across an initialisation file supplied with a piece of software that has been designed by the software vendor not to be editable. For various reasons, the file is normally designed not to be opened or modified except through the controls built into the software vendor's specific application. Do not be alarmed then, if whilst experimenting, you attempt to open an INI file and find that you cannot, for it is probably not corrupted or in error.

CHAPTER

4

PROGRAM INFORMATION FILES (PIFS)

Windows 3 and Windows 3.1 do not use PIFs as extensively as previous versions of Windows. If you have used older versions of Windows, you will note that after installing Windows there is no PIF sub-directory with dozens of PIFs. Windows can now run just about any non-Windows application without a PIF.

This is made possible because Windows no longer attempts to run a non-Windows application in a window. In Real or Standard mode the only way to run a non-Windows application is to switch it to full screen.

Most applications now run with the same default settings found in _DEFAULT.PIF. You will find that with Windows 3.x, PIFs are used to fine tune settings for improved performance rather than to make it possible for non-Windows applications to run. Program Information Files are also used to control the environment that non-Windows programs execute in when running under the control of Windows.

The type of video support and memory requirements are two of the many settings that can be tailored to enhance the stability and performance of programs.

REAL AND STANDARD MODE

Windows does not support the multi-tasking of non-Windows programs in Real and Standard mode. One non-Windows program can run full screen with the others being kept in a suspended state in the background.

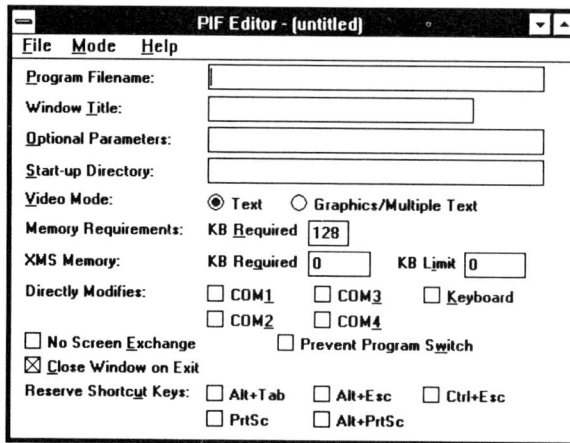

Figure 4.1 Windows 3.0 Real and Standard mode PIF EDITOR.

The following is a description of each option available in the Real and Standard mode PIF EDITOR.

Program Filename (Mandatory)

In this box enter the name of the program or batch file that you want the PIF to execute. The name can contain the full path if required.

For example, to run WordPerfect 5.1 directly you would type:

```
C:\WP51\WP.EXE
```

or, if you use a batch file the entry would be:

C:\BATS\WP.BAT

Windows Title (Optional)

Use this setting to specify the title that is to be placed under the program icon when it is minimised. If you leave the box blank the name of the program's filename will be used.

Optional Parameters (Optional)

Certain MS DOS programs can be supplied with parameters when run. For example, it is possible to supply the name of a source file that is to be loaded and executed when GW-BASIC is started.

The information entered here can be any combination of up to 62 characters. One special feature is the ? parameter, which causes Windows to request parameters each time the program is started.

Start-up Directory (Optional)

This entry tells Windows the directory to start the program in. If the program you are trying to run needs access to a configuration file before it can start, an entry will probably have to be made here.

Video Mode (Mandatory)

This option tells Windows the amount of memory to set aside for the storing of the program's display. If the program you are going to run executes in text mode i.e. it does not generate graphics, select the TEXT option. Otherwise use the GRAPHICS/MULTIPLE TEXT option.

The memory to store the screen is taken from memory allocated to the program. If you select the GRAPHICS/MULTIPLE TEXT option for a text only program you are depriving your program of space that it can use for data storage.

If you select the incorrect setting Windows will stop you switching away from the program. The only way to return to Windows will be to terminate the program.

Memory Requirements, KB Required (Mandatory)

This parameter informs Windows of the amount of conventional memory that needs to be available in order to start the program. The default setting is 128K.
This entry does NOT specify the amount of conventional memory that should be allocated to a program by Windows. When the program starts Windows gives it all the available conventional memory in the system.

If Windows does not have enough conventional memory free to start the program a dialog box will be displayed. You will then have to close other programs to release memory.

XMS Memory (Optional)

If your program is able to make use of extended memory that conforms to the Lotus-Intel-Microsoft eXtended Memory Specification (XMS) enter the amount that your program needs in the boxes provided.

In the box labelled KB REQUIRED specify the amount of XMS memory that must be free in order for the program to start. The recommended value for this entry is zero. A value greater than zero will dramatically increase the time it takes to switch to and from the program.

The other box, labelled KB LIMIT is used to control the amount of extended memory the program has access to. A value of -1 tells Windows to provide the program with all the extended memory it requests (up to the maximum available). A value of zero prevents the program from using extended memory.

Directly Modifies (Optional)

Use these settings if your program requires the exclusive control of the keyboard or communication ports when it is running. Examples are communications packages such as ProComm Plus.

By selecting the KEYBOARD option, Windows will be stopped from responding to any shortcut keys, for example, CTRL+ESC to select the TASK LIST. This means that the only way to leave the program will be to exit it. More conventional memory can be made available to your program by selecting the KEYBOARD option.

No Screen Exchange (Optional)

This option stops the screen from being copied to the CLIPBOARD when the PRINT SCREEN key is pressed. Conventional memory can be conserved by disabling the SCREEN EXCHANGE function.

Prevent Program Switch (Optional)

Selecting this option stops you switching away from the application once it has started. The only way to leave the application is to exit in the normal way. Once again conventional memory can be saved through the use of this option.

Close Window on Exit (Optional)

This option tells Windows whether it should close the programs window and return control to Windows when the application is exited. If this option is not selected, you will be shown a message when you try to leave the program telling you to press a key to return to Windows.

Reserve Shortcut Keys (Optional)

Some applications make use of the special Windows shortcut key combinations. For instance a 3270 emulator may use the PRINT SCREEN key to send a screen dump to the printer. To stop Windows intercepting the key combinations, you can disable it by placing a cross in the box next to the combination.

In the previous example, the placing of a cross next to the PRTSC option will ensure screen dumps go to the printer and not the Windows CLIPBOARD.

386 ENHANCED MODE

Due to the increased functionality of Windows when it is running in 386 Enhanced mode, a number of new options become available in the PIF editor. The options available are split into two groups; BASIC and ADVANCED. The BASIC set of options are similar to those in Real and Standard mode whereas the ADVANCED options allow you to configure the type of memory that should be made available to the application, and its priority when multi-tasking.

Program Filename (Mandatory)

For details see the description in the Real and Standard mode section earlier in this chapter.

Windows Title (Optional)

For details see the description in the Real and Standard mode section earlier in this chapter.

Optional Parameters (Optional)

For details see the description in the Real and Standard mode section earlier in this chapter.

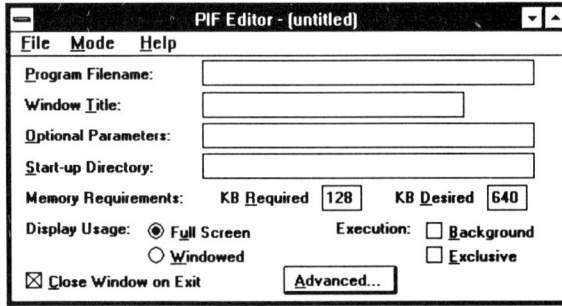

Figure 4.2 Windows PIF EDITOR BASIC options in 386 Enhanced mode.

Start-up Directory (Optional)

For details see the description in the Real and Standard mode section earlier in this chapter.

Memory Requirements (Mandatory)

These options are used to tell Windows the amount of conventional memory the program requires when running. The first parameter, KB REQUIRED, specifies the amount of conventional memory that must be free in order for the application to start. The second parameter, KB DESIRED, specifies the maximum amount of conventional memory that Windows should allocate to the program, up to a maximum of 640K.

You can tell Windows to give the application as much conventional memory as possible (up to 640K) by placing a -1 in both boxes.

N.B. **The default settings (128K and 640K) are valid for most applications. Memory can be saved, for use with other programs, by reducing these values. For example, a Banyan VINES 3270 session can function quite happily with 256K (see Chapter 12 on Banyan VINES).**

Display Usage (Mandatory)

This setting tells Windows to run the program either in a window or full screen when it is started. Once the application has begun to run it is possible to toggle between the two modes by pressing the ALT+ENTER keys together.

Execution (Optional)

These options are used to control the way a program runs. The BACKGROUND setting instructs Windows to keep the application executing in the background when you are using another application. The BACKGROUND setting is important when using communication programs such as VINES 3270. To maintain a link with the mainframe at all times ensure that this box has a cross entered in it.

The other option, EXCLUSIVE, instructs Windows to suspend all other programs (irrespective of whether they have their BACKGROUND options selected) when this program is running. The EXCLUSIVE option can provide the program with more memory and processor time.

Only use the EXCLUSIVE option as a last resort. You may find that you need to use it when running a 3270 session if your connection keeps being dropped.

Close Windows on Exit (Optional)

For details see the description in the Real and Standard mode section earlier in this chapter.

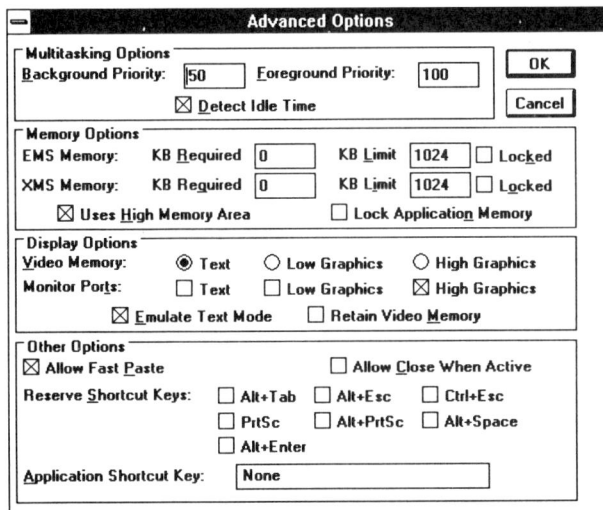

Figure 4.3 Windows PIF EDITOR ADVANCED options in 386 Enhanced mode.

Multi-Tasking Options (Mandatory)

These options are used to control the amount of processor time that an application should receive in relation to other tasks currently running. The values entered in the BACKGROUND and FOREGROUND boxes range from 1 to 10000.

The value in the BACKGROUND box is ignored if the BACKGROUND option in the EXECUTION section of the BASIC options has not been selected. By setting the DETECT IDLE TIME switch, Windows can make further processor time available to other applications when it believes that your program is in an idle state, for example, waiting for input.

Memory Options (Mandatory)

Windows running in 386 Enhanced mode only uses extended memory (see appendix B for a full description of PC memory). Expanded memory is simulated using extended memory for those programs that need it.

As with the conventional memory requirements set in the BASIC options the KB REQUIRED boxes specify the amount of expanded (EMS) and/or extended (XMS) memory that needs to be available in order for the program to start. The KB LIMIT box, as before, specifies the maximum amount of EMS and/or XMS that can be made available to the program. Placing a -1 in these boxes tells Windows to allocate as much memory as the program asks for.

If your program does not use either EMS and/or XMS then set both settings to zero. This will save valuable memory for use with other programs, and allow you to run more concurrent tasks within the memory available in your machine.

The HIGH MEMORY AREA (HMA) is the first 64K of extended memory. By setting this switch on a further 64K of memory can be made available to those programs that are able to make use of it. If you use a Terminate and Stay-Resident (TSR) utility or network driver software that loads itself into the HMA before you start Windows, this option should not be used.

The LOCKED switches prohibits Windows from swapping the conventional, expanded and extended memory to disk. The program execution speed can be increased by setting these options; however, the overall performance of your Windows environment will be decreased. The recommended setting for the LOCKED switches is off.

Display Options (Mandatory)

These options are used to inform Windows of the amount of memory it needs to provide in order to store a programs display. The higher the setting selected, the more memory Windows will allocate.

MODE	MEMORY USED
Text	Up to 16K.
Low graphics (CGA)	32K.
High graphics (EGA/VGA)	128K.

The MONITOR PORTS settings are for programs that access the video hardware directly. Before setting one of these switches try your program with them all set to off. As Windows has to monitor your application when one of these is set, system performance can be reduced.

The EMULATE TEXT MODE switch when set may speed up the displaying of text by your program. To ensure maximum performance for your programs always set this switch on. If your screen is corrupted then set this switch off.

Once a program has started, Windows is able to dynamically alter the amount of memory allocated for its display as it changes display mode. Setting the RETAIN VIDEO MEMORY switch will stop this and ensure that your program will not run out of video memory. The recommended setting is off. However if you find that your display is being corrupted you may need to set the switch on.

Other Options (Optional)

The settings in this section are similar to the options available in Real and Standard mode. Due to the increased functionality of Windows in 386 Enhanced mode there are a couple of points of interest.

CLOSE WHEN ACTIVE when set allows you to leave a program without having to select its exit command. The recommended setting for this switch is off as unpredictable results may occur by incorrectly terminating a program.

In 386 Enhanced mode Windows provides a method of selecting a program by a key combination. For instance, you could assign ALT+M to automatically select your electronic mail application. Enter your key combinations in the APPLICATION SHORTCUT KEY box, but be careful of conflicts with other programs and Windows key combinations.

PIF PRIORITY

With Windows in 386 Enhanced mode the user is able to control how much time is to be allocated to each application when more than one is running at the same time. These priorities are given when creating the PIF file for that particular application and using the foreground and background priority fields.

For example, suppose a user has three applications running. One application is running in the foreground with a foreground priority of 100. The other two are running in the background and each has a background priority of 40. The total priority of all applications is 180 (100 + 40 + 40). Of this total, the foreground application will receive 100 out of the 180 (or 55%) of the processor's time, and each of the background tasks will receive 22% each.

CHAPTER

5

GENERAL DOS CONSIDERATIONS

Windows is a very powerful graphical environment but it should be remembered that, at least at present, it runs on top of DOS and as such is technically an operating environment rather than a fully fledged operating system in its own right. As a result of all this and because users will most probably still want to access DOS applications there are a number of factors which need to be considered regarding DOS.

Chapter 6 discusses MS-DOS 5 which can be used successfully with Windows. This chapter deals with general DOS considerations that can apply to most versions (and makes) of DOS.

DOS IN A WINDOW

If you are running in 386 Enhanced mode, it is possible to run your MS-DOS session in a window. Users of Windows version 3.0 should create a program information file and give it a meaningful name, something like COMMAND.PIF, MSDOS.PIF or DRDOS.PIF - depending on the DOS you are using. Set the DISPLAY USAGE option to WINDOWED. Whenever you click on the DOS prompt icon, COMMAND.COM will receive control and start in a window rather than full-screen.

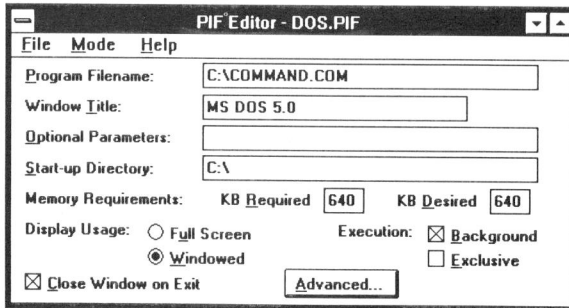

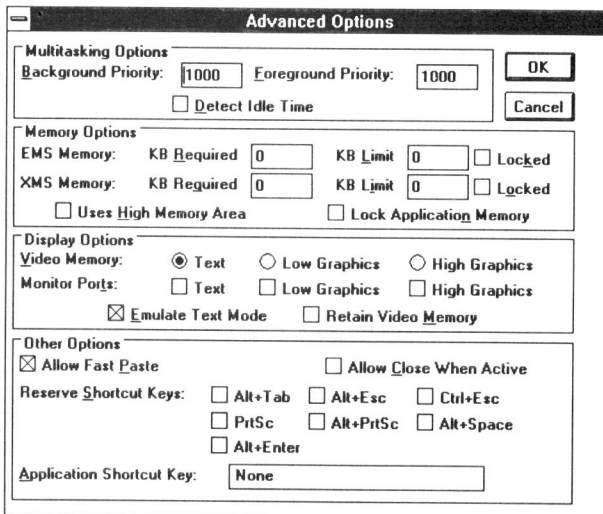

Figure 5.1 PIF settings for a windowed MS-DOS session.

They should also ensure that the Execution: Background switch is set. When using 386 Enhanced mode, this will allow you to switch away from an executing DOS application and continue to do something else in Windows whilst the DOS application continues to run.

Windows version 3.1 is supplied with a DOS program information file, DOSPRMPT.PIF. This provides the same functionality as the one we have just shown you how to create.

To demonstrate the benefits of background DOS execution using a PIF try the following for yourself. Open up a DOS window and either format a blank floppy disk or perhaps Copy a large number of files from your hard drive to the floppy drive. Once this operation is under way, you will be given some indication as to the extent of the operation that has so far completed - keep an eye on this. Then swap away from this DOS application, using either the mouse to click on another window or using an Alt+Esc or Ctrl+Esc keyboard sequence. Whilst moving to another application you should see the DOS Format or Copy operation continuing - this is multi-tasking and the result of Background execution.

DOS PROMPT

Have you ever used a full-screen DOS session to execute a few commands only to forget that you are running Windows? By building the small batch file shown in figure 5.2 you will not only be reminded that you are still in Windows, you will also be given the opportunity to load some of your DOS TSRs or utilities for use in your DOS session.

```
@ECHO OFF
PROMPT [W] $P$G
REM *** Load your TSR or utilities here... ***
COMMAND.COM
```

Figure 5.2 Batch file to remind user that he is still in Windows

the PROMPT command will make your DOS session (for example from the WINDOWS sub-directory) look like this:

```
[W] C:\WINDOWS> _
```

The idea being that the [W] before the filespec will remind users that they need to type EXIT to return to Windows. If you load any TSRs in the batch file in figure 5.2 they will automatically be removed from memory when you leave your DOS session.

ICONS FOR DOS APPLICATIONS

Windows version 3.0 allowed you to associate any icon with a DOS application (whilst it was in the Program Manager). However, as soon as you ran the application, and then either minimised or switched away from it, you would lose that icon and be presented with the standard Microsoft DOS application icon in its place.

This has changed with Windows version 3.1, and any icon you associate with a DOS application will remain with it. Remember that there are a large number of 'Hidden Icons' supplied with Windows for you to use - a section in Chapter 9, Miscellaneous Hints and Tips, tells you how to find and use them.

KEYBOARD SPEED SETTING

The Windows CONTROL PANEL contains a single keyboard speed setting. PC keyboards have two settings: initial delay and repeat rate. Unfortunately you will find that the CONTROL PANEL will set the initial delay so that the response to keys is slow.

You can solve this by using your own keyboard speed setting program. Put your program in your AUTOEXEC.BAT file and then disable the Windows keyboard speed setting by removing the following line from the WIN.INI file.

    KeyboardSpeed=

It is best if your keyboard setting program is the kind that just sets the speed in the keyboard hardware rather than a program that stays resident and uses timer interrupts. Be careful, as there is just one problem with getting Windows to leave your speed setting alone. If you ever click on the KEYBOARD icon in the CONTROL PANEL, Windows will go back to its own setting - even if you cancel out of the dialog box.

DOS UTILITIES TO AVOID

Some DOS utilities can cause problems when used in conjunction with Windows. They are:

APPEND
JOIN
SUBST

If you have included any of these in your AUTOEXEC.BAT file, remove them and refrain from using them with Windows.

CHKDSK

The DOS CHKDSK utility is used to provide statistics about your computer's memory and hard disk. One of its options is to repair damaged files on your hard disk (CHKDSK /F). This process will update the File Allocation Table (FAT) of DOS and can cause conflicts if run under Windows.

N.B.   Always run CHKDSK outside of your Windows environment.

THE DOS SHARE UTILITY

If you wish to prevent more than one application from modifying the same file, you can use the DOS utility SHARE.EXE (normally used in a network environment where files may be shared between users).

With SHARE installed, all read and write requests of an application are validated against the file sharing code in which the file was opened. The SHARE command (in an AUTOEXEC.BAT) accepts the following switches:

    /F:space /L:locks

where SPACE defaults to 2048 and is the size of a storage area used to record file sharing information, and LOCKS defaults to 20, and is the number of locks you want to allow. SHARE will only work correctly if you run it before starting Windows (do not try to run it from within Windows).

ENVIRONMENT SPACE

Greater demands are placed upon the environment space of DOS when running Windows, especially in a local area network environment. The SHELL statement in the CONFIG.SYS file is used to set the size of DOS' environment.

The default size for the environment space is 256 bytes and this is taken out of conventional memory. Figure 5.3 shows the command line required to set the environment size to 1K (1024 bytes).

```
SHELL=C:\DOS\COMMAND.COM C:\ /P /E:1024
```

Figure 5.3 Setting the MS-DOS environment size via the SHELL command.

You will know when you have found the correct setting as the dreaded 'Out of environment space' errors will go away. The environment can be anywhere between 256 to 32,768 bytes in size. On networked PCs we have found a value of 2,048 bytes is required.

PREVENTING STACK OVERFLOW

Stacks are temporary data structures that MS-DOS and applications use for processing hardware interrupt events. If you receive the 'Internal Stack Overflow' message when you are running Windows in 386 Enhanced mode, you need to change the STACKS setting in your CONFIG.SYS file.

If your system uses MS-DOS 3.2, include the following line:

```
STACKS=9,192
```

If your system uses MS-DOS 3.3 or 4.01, include the following line:

```
STACKS=0,0
```

If your system uses MS-DOS 5.0, include the following line:

```
STACKS=9,128
```

It is a good idea to include these statements in any CONFIG.SYS files you create to prevent these error messages ever occurring. The STACKS=0,0 option also increases the performance of MS-DOS 3.3/4.01.

CHOOSING A VERSION OF DOS

There are currently four flavours of DOS to choose from, which are:

(1) MS-DOS version 3.3.

+ Stable version.
+ Works with all software.
+ Smaller conventional memory footprint.
- Does not support disk partitions greater than 32MB.
- No advanced features such as on-line help.

(2) MS-DOS version 4.01.

+ The ability to support disk partitions larger than 32MB.
+ Expanded memory support.
+ Enhanced batch file commands.
+ A user interface shell.
- Uses up large amount of conventional memory.
- Contains bugs and has an untrustworthy reputation.

(3) MS-DOS version 5.0.

+ Advanced memory management.
+ Enhanced support for Windows.
+ New full screen editor.
+ On-line help.
+ Editable command line.
+ Clever disk utilities such as UNDELETE.
- Stability not yet proven.

(4) DR-DOS version 5.0 (and 6.0).

+ Advanced memory management.
+ New full screen editor.
+ On-line help.
+ Editable command line.
+ Disk compression (version 6.0 only).
- Memory manager not Windows compatible (v5.0 only).
- Not written by Microsoft.

From our own experiences we recommend MS-DOS 5. The benefits to Windows users come in the form of increased performance (due mainly to the increased amount of available conventional memory) and excellent stability.

If you want to wait until MS-DOS 5 has been around for a while and 'proved' itself then we recommend MS-DOS 3.3 or DR-DOS 5.0 and a memory manager such as 386MAX or QEMM386.

Digital Research have also released DR-DOS version 6.0 which might be worth considering once it has 'settled down'.

CHAPTER

6

MICROSOFT MS-DOS 5.0

Several years ago, IBM and Microsoft thought that, with the arrival of an advanced operating system such as OS/2, users would naturally migrate on from DOS. This clearly did not happen and as we can see today, DOS is alive and well and (at least for the next 12 months) is still the underlying basis for the Microsoft Windows operating environment.

Microsoft sensibly changed their plans and strategies when they realised people were not going to change to OS/2 in large numbers and are now even more firmly committed to supporting and enhancing DOS. There are an estimated 60 million copies of DOS in the world and Microsoft ship another 18 million copies every year. This easily makes DOS the best selling piece of software in the world.

MS-DOS 5.0 sets out to dramatically reduce the footprint of DOS in conventional memory (see appendix B for a full description of the different types of PC memory) and achieves this by using the advanced hardware features of the Intel range of 32 bit microprocessors. It is possible to relocate device drivers, TSRs (Terminate and Stay Resident programs) and even DOS itself to memory above the 640K line, thus providing applications with well over 600K of conventional memory in which to execute.

INSTALLATION OF MS-DOS 5.0

The installation procedure of MS-DOS 5.0 is very simple. Unfortunately this simplicity means that users are left to edit the AUTOEXEC.BAT and CONFIG.SYS files manually if they wish to take advantage of the new features such as advanced memory management and the command line history.

The impression given is that in their rush to get MS-DOS 5.0 on to the market Microsoft did not spend much time in developing an intelligent installation program. Certainly installation and ease of tailorability are two areas where Digital Research DOS 5.0 is streets ahead of Microsoft.

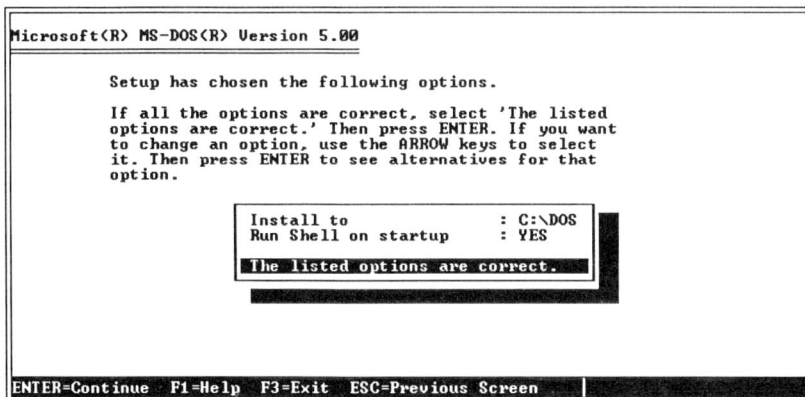

```
Microsoft(R) MS-DOS(R) Version 5.00

        Setup has chosen the following options.

        If all the options are correct, select 'The listed
        options are correct.' Then press ENTER. If you want
        to change an option, use the ARROW keys to select
        it. Then press ENTER to see alternatives for that
        option.

            ┌─────────────────────────────────────────┐
            │ Install to             : C:\DOS          │
            │ Run Shell on startup   : YES             │
            │ The listed options are correct.          │
            └─────────────────────────────────────────┘


ENTER=Continue  F1=Help  F3=Exit  ESC=Previous Screen
```

Figure 6.1 MS-DOS 5.0 installation program.

ENHANCED MS-DOS 5.0 FUNCTIONALITY

Although it is obvious that Microsoft's main objective with MS-DOS 5.0 was to improve DOS' memory management facilities, they have taken the time to include some very useful extensions to the MS-DOS standard with this release.

The most notable improvements are:

o   Advanced memory management.
o   Increased performance for Windows 3 users.
o   On-line help for DOS commands.
o   Editable DOS command line and history.
o   Full screen text editor to replace EDLIN.
o   New and enhanced DOS commands such as UNDELETE and
    UNFORMAT.
o   New powerful DOS shell providing task switching.
o   New version of BASIC called Quick BASIC.
o   Support for 2GB disk partitions and 2.88MB 3.5" floppy disks.

Advanced MS-DOS 5.0 Memory Management

To fully utilise the advanced memory management features of MS-
DOS 5.0 an understanding of the different types of PC memory is
required.   Appendix B in this book is a useful starting point and
chapter 12 in the *MS-DOS 5.0 User's Guide and Reference* deals
specifically with the tools that MS-DOS 5.0 provides.

In brief, MS-DOS 5.0 is supplied with an extended memory
manager and an expanded memory emulator.   Their purpose, in
addition to providing access to these two types of memory, is to
allow the relocating of device drivers, TSRs and DOS into the upper
memory area (memory between 640K and 1MB).

Two new DOS commands, LOADHIGH and DEVICEHIGH, can be
used in the AUTOEXEC.BAT and CONFIG.SYS files respectively
to load programs and device drivers into upper memory.
Unfortunately the method for activating the upper memory facilities
is not clearly explained in the MS-DOS 5.0 manual and many
frustrating hours can be spent, often with little success.

The following is a clear (we hope!) step by step guide to accessing the upper memory area of a PC using MS-DOS 5.0.

(1) Insert the following line in the CONFIG.SYS file.

```
DEVICE=C:\HIMEM.SYS
```

HIMEM.SYS is an extended memory manager providing access to the memory above 1MB.   As with the version of HIMEM.SYS provided with Windows 3 it is possible to specify the type of A20 memory handler to be used via the /MACHINE switch. Possible values are shown in figure 6.2.

(2) Insert the following line in the CONFIG.SYS file.

```
DEVICE=C:\MSDOS5\EMM386.EXE NOEMS
```

The EMM386 driver can be used for two purposes; the first is to provide a page frame for access to expanded memory in the upper memory area, and the other is to enable support for upper memory blocks (UMBs) which are used to relocate device drivers and TSRs into.

There are a number of parameters which can be specified after EMM386.EXE but the two which are important if you want to use the relocation features of MS-DOS 5.0 are RAM and NOEMS.

The RAM parameter informs EMM386 to emulate expanded memory using extended memory and to provide access to UMBs. The disadvantage of this option is that 64K of the upper memory area is used for the expanded memory page frame.

SETTING	MACHINE
1	IBM PC/AT Compuadd 386 systems JDR 386/33
2	IBM PS/2 Datamedia 386/486 Unisys Power Port
3	Phoenix Cascade BIOS
4	HP Vectra (A and A+)
5	AT&T 6300 Plus
6	Acer 1100
7	Toshiba 1600 Toshiba 1200XE Toshiba 5100
8	Wyse 12.5MHz 286 Compuadd 386 systems Hitachi HL500C Intel 301z or 302
9	Tulip SX
10	Zenith ZBIOS
11	IBM PC/AT
12	IBM PC/AT (alternative delay) CSS Labs
13	IBM PC/AT (alternative delay) Philips
14	HP Vectra
16	Bull Micral 60

Figure 6.2 Possible values for the A20 memory handler.

The other parameter, NOEMS, also provides access to UMBs but turns off the expanded memory emulation thus increasing the amount of upper memory free by 64K. The extra 64K will be useful if you intend to relocate a large device driver such as a network driver.

(3) Insert the following line in the CONFIG.SYS file.

```
DOS=HIGH,UMB
```

This command instructs MS-DOS 5.0 to relocate the MS-DOS kernel to the high memory area (HMA) and to maintain a link between conventional memory and the upper memory area so that relocation of device drivers and TSRs is possible.

After the above three steps have been completed the DEVICEHIGH and LOADHIGH commands can be used to relocate device drivers such as SMARTDRV.SYS and KEYBOARD.SYS. It is not unreasonable to expect the MEM command to report in excess of 610K of free conventional memory.

The MEM utility provided with MS-DOS 5.0 is capable of supplying details of the size and location of device drivers and TSRs in memory. Figure 6.3 shows the depth of information that can be provided by the MEM command.

The following advice will be useful when trying to find an optimum configuration.

(1) Use the MEM command to find out the size of the device drivers and TSRs that are to be installed. Once a list has been compiled load them into upper memory in size order (largest first). This method of loading will ensure the most efficient use of upper memory.

(2) If the SMARTDRIVE disk cache utility provided with MS-DOS 5.0 is being used, insert a BUFFERS=1,1 statement in the

CONFIG.SYS file. This sets the number of buffers to the minimum and saves conventional memory.

(3) Insert a LASTDRIVE statement in the CONFIG.SYS file with a value equal to the highest DOS drive available, for example, LASTDRIVE=C. Each drive allocation requires 100 bytes and so over specification is wasteful.

```
Conventional Memory :

    Name            Size in Decimal          Size in Hex
    -----------     -------------------      ------------

    MSDOS           14384     ( 14.0K)          3830
    HIMEM            1184     (  1.2K)           4A0
    EMM386           9424     (  9.2K)          24D0
    COMMAND          4416     (  4.3K)          1140
    FREE               64     (  0.1K)            40
    FREE           625680     (611.0K)         98C10

Total   FREE :     625744     (611.1K)

Upper Memory :

    Name            Size in Decimal          Size in Hex
    -----------     -------------------      ------------

    SYSTEM         163840     (160.0K)         28000
    SMARTDRV        21952     ( 21.4K)          55C0
    MOUSE           14816     ( 14.5K)          39E0
    SETVER            400     (  0.4K)           190
    KEYB             6208     (  6.1K)          1840
    DOSKEY           4128     (  4.0K)          1020
    FREE              176     (  0.2K)            B0
    FREE            50480     ( 49.3K)          C530

Total   FREE :      50656     ( 49.5K)

Total bytes available to programs (Conventional+Upper) :   676400    (660.5K)
Largest executable program size :                          625488    (610.8K)
Largest available upper memory block :                      50480    ( 49.3K)

    3145728 bytes total contiguous extended memory
          0 bytes available contiguous extended memory
    1846272 bytes available XMS memory
            MS-DOS resident in High Memory Area
```

Figure 6.3 Example output from the MEM command.

(4) If the software you intend to run does not require file control blocks insert an FCBS=1 statement in the CONFIG.SYS file. This FCBS setting will save about 50 bytes of conventional memory.

(5) If the machine running MS-DOS 5.0 is an XT type machine (i.e. it has an Intel 8088 or 8086 microprocessor), add a STACKS=0,0 statement to the CONFIG.SYS file. For AT class machines (those with an Intel 80286 or above microprocessor) add a STACKS=9,128 statement.

(6) To search out every last available byte of upper memory you will require a PC memory analysis tool. Although it is possible to buy such tools, one which we strongly recommend is called ASQ. ASQ is written by Qualitas (the people who created 386MAX) and is available free of charge from many good public domain libraries. ASQ also includes a comprehensive tutorial on all aspects of tuning your PC configuration.

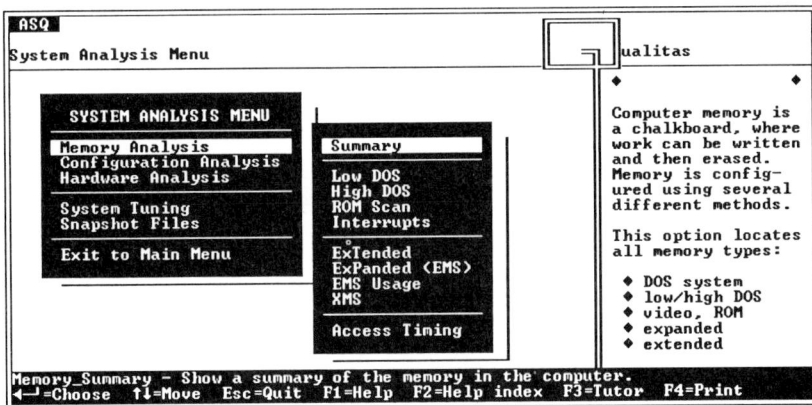

Figure 6.4 ASQ from Qualitas.

Any upper memory that ASQ reports as unused can be reclaimed for use by MS-DOS 5.0 by adding an include parameter to the EMM386 command line in the CONFIG.SYS file. Figure 6.5 shows how a 64K segment of upper memory block at address E000-F000 can be reclaimed.

```
DEVICE=C:\MSDOS5\EMM386.EXE NOEMS I=E000-F000
```

Figure 6.5 Example of the include parameter for the EMM386 utility.

Some hardware devices fitted to PCs such as LAN cards usually use a small area of upper memory as a communications area. To stop MS-DOS 5.0 corrupting this memory an exclude parameter needs to be added to the EMM386 command line. Figure 6.6 shows the command line required to exclude 8K of memory used by a LAN card at address CC000.

```
DEVICE=C:\MSDOS5\EMM386.EXE NOEMS I=E000-F000 X=CC00-CE00
```

Figure 6.6 Example of the exclude parameter for the EMM386 utility.

Remember that Windows also checks all available memory when it starts up, specifically looking for used portions of memory in the upper memory area. Any used areas of memory can also be excluded via EMMEXCLUDE entries in SYSTEM.INI.

Windows 3 Considerations

The new versions of HIMEM.SYS, SMARTDRV.SYS and EMM386.EXE supplied with MS-DOS 5.0 are all of special interest to users of Windows 3. They have been optimised to link DOS more closely with Windows and as a result the performance of Windows 3 increases significantly.

If you are installing MS-DOS 5.0 on to a machine that is already running Windows ensure that your CONFIG.SYS file is pointing to the new versions in the MS-DOS directory.

If you install Windows 3 after MS-DOS 5.0 the Windows installation program will alter the CONFIG.SYS file so that it points to the versions supplied with Windows rather than the ones supplied with MS-DOS 5.0.

```
DEVICE=C:\MSDOS5\HIMEM.SYS
DEVICE=C:\MSDOS5\EMM386.EXE ...
DEVICE=C:\MSDOS5\SMARTDRV.SYS ...
```

Figure 6.7 CONFIG.SYS after the installation of MS-DOS 5.0

```
DEVICE=C:\HIMEM.SYS
DEVICE=C:\WINDOWS\EMM386.SYS ...
DEVICE=C:\WINDOWS\SMARTDRV.SYS ...
```

Figure 6.8 CONFIG.SYS after the installation of Windows 3.

To use the MS-DOS 5.0 drivers, once more edit the CONFIG.SYS file and alter the lines shown in figure 6.7 to be the same as those in figure 6.8. Save the CONFIG.SYS file and re-boot your machine.

The WINA20.386 File

The MS-DOS 5.0 SETUP routine places the (read-only) file WINA20.386 in the root directory during installation. This file is needed by Windows if the user wishes to run in 386 Enhanced mode.

Windows will either not run in 386 Enhanced mode under MS-DOS 5.0 without it or at the very best it will intermittently hang.

The A20 address line is a feature of the Intel386 and Intel486 microprocessors and is briefly described in Appendix B, PC Memory Explained when discussing the High Memory Area.

Many users want to keep their hard drives well organised and hardly want a file such as this cluttering up their root directory. If you are like this then you will wish to move the file somewhere else. We suggest you place it in either the sub-directory where you installed MS-DOS 5.0 or where you installed Windows.

However, when you move it you must indicate to DOS that it should (i) let Windows search for and load this file and (ii) indicate to Windows where it can now find the file. If you do not do this you will receive an error message something like "You must have the file WINA20.386 in the root of your boot drive to run Windows in Enhanced mode". This is done by:

(1) Adding a SWITCHES=/W command to your CONFIG.SYS file.

(2) Adding a DEVICE=[drive:][path]]WINA20.386 command to the [386Enh] section of your Windows SYSTEM.INI file.

On-line Help for DOS Commands

Have you ever forgotten the syntax of an MS-DOS command? Well help (excuse the pun) is now available via the question mark (?) switch and the MS-DOS 5.0 HELP command. The information presented by both options is the same; it is simply a matter of choice which you use.

Figure 6.9 shows the information presented by MS-DOS 5.0 when HELP BACKUP is typed at the MS-DOS prompt.

```
C:>HELP BACKUP
```

backs up one or more files from one disk to another.

Entering the HELP command without any parameters will produce a list of all the MS-DOS 5.0 commands along with a brief description of each. The online help functionality does not use any conventional memory and is always available, i.e. it cannot be turned off.

```
BACKUP source destination-drive: [/S] [/M] [/A] [/F[:size]]
  [/D:date[/T:time]] [/L[:[drive:][path]logfile]]

  source               Specifies the file(s), drive, or directory to back up.
  destination-drive:   Specifies the drive to save backup copies onto.
  /S                   Backs up contents of subdirectories.
  /M                   Backs up only files that have changed since the last
                       backup.
  /A                   Adds backup files to an existing backup disk.
  /F:[size]            Specifies the size of the disk to be formatted.
  /D:date              Backs up only files changed on or after the specified
                       date.
  /T:time              Backs up only files changed at or after the specified
                       time.
  /L[:[drive:][path]logfile]
                       Creates a log file and entry to record the backup
                       operation.
```

Figure 6.9 MS-DOS 5.0 help information for the BACKUP command.

Editable DOS Command Lines

A utility program called DOSKEY is supplied with MS-DOS 5.0 which allows DOS command lines to be recalled and edited. To run the program insert the line in figure 6.9 into your AUTOEXEC.BAT file. If you have sufficient free space in upper memory DOSKEY can be loaded above 640K by prefixing the line with the LOADHIGH command.

```
C:\MSDOS5\DOSKEY /INSERT
```

Figure 6.10 AUTOEXEC.BAT command line needed to run DOSKEY.

The line in figure 6.10 provides DOSKEY with a default command line buffer size of 512 bytes, which should store approximately thirty lines. The /INSERT switch allows characters to be inserted when editing a command line rather than the default setting of overtype. For a full description of all options that can be used with DOSKEY read Chapter 7, Advanced Command Techniques, in the *MS-DOS 5.0 User's Guide and Reference*.

The New Full Screen MS-DOS 5.0 Editor

The new editor supplied with MS-DOS 5.0 has finally made DOS' infamous EDLIN utility redundant. The new program, based on the Quick BASIC editor, has pull-down menus, online help and can be controlled with a mouse. To use a mouse with the editor a suitable mouse driver, such as MOUSE.SYS needs to loaded in the CONFIG.SYS file (the mouse driver can be loaded into upper memory to save conventional memory).

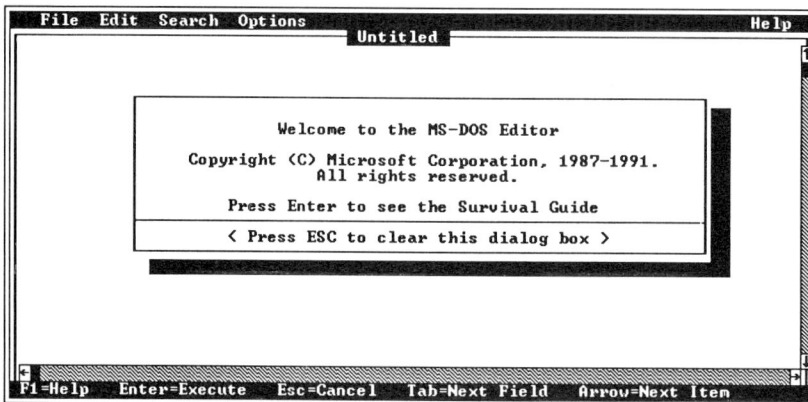

Figure 6.11 MS-DOS 5.0 editor.

New and Enhanced MS-DOS 5.0 Commands

DIR

The functionality of the DIR command has been enhanced to include the ability to search for files, sort the output and also via the AUTOEXEC.BAT command alter the default settings.

By suffixing the DIR command with the /O switch it is possible to obtain a sorted directory listing. The ordering can be controlled with the following switches:

n	Ascending filename order (A through Z).
-n	Descending filename order (Z through A).
e	Ascending filename extension order.
-e	Descending filename extension order.
d	Ascending date order.
-d	Descending date order.
s	Ascending size order.
-s	Descending size order.
g	Directories before files.
-g	Directories after files.

Figure 6.12 shows the use of the -n switch on the DIR command, producing a directory listing with the filenames listed in descending order.

Another useful feature of the DIR command is its ability to search for files. By suffixing the command with /S a search is made of the current directory and all the sub-directories for files that match the supplied pattern. For example, if DIR *.TXT /S was entered whilst in the root directory, a search of the entire disk would be made for any files with an extension type of TXT.

Finally, it is possible to alter the default settings of the DIR command through the use of the SET DIRCMD option in the AUTOEXEC.BAT file. If you would like your DIR command always to produce directory listings across rather than down the screen, entering SET DIRCMD=/W in the AUTOEXEC.BAT file will achieve this.

```
C:>DIR /O:-N

Volume in drive C is PADDY-0691
Volume Serial Number is 16E6-8BDC
Directory of C:\

WINSDL          <DIR>      24/06/91    20:55
WINDOWS         <DIR>      03/06/91     1:08
WINA20   386         9349  09/04/91     5:00
WEP             <DIR>      03/06/91     1:12
PSFONTS         <DIR>      03/06/91     1:13
PRODPACK        <DIR>      03/06/91     1:12
PCPLUS          <DIR>      03/06/91     1:11
MSMOUSE         <DIR>      06/07/91    21:22
MSDOS5          <DIR>      06/07/91    17:30
M7000           <DIR>      24/06/91    20:07
ICONS           <DIR>      08/06/91    21:57
HIMEM    SYS       11552   09/04/91     5:00
FASTBACK        <DIR>      03/06/91     1:11
EXCEL           <DIR>      23/06/91    16:26
CONFIG   SYS        1454   21/07/91    15:57
COMMAND  COM       47845   09/04/91     5:00
AUTOEXEC BAT        1592   21/07/91    11:59
ASQ             <DIR>      13/07/91     0:05
        18 file(s)          70483 bytes
                         48300032 bytes free
```

Figure 6.12 Example output from the DIR command using the -n order switch.

FORMAT

Two new switches have been added to the FORMAT command:

/Q   This will perform a 'quick' format of the destination disk. It can only be used on disks that have already been formatted and will delete and recreate the MS-DOS file allocation table (FAT). It is advisable that this command only be used on disks which are known to be free of defects.

/U   This will perform an unconditional format. Any data on the disk is destroyed and cannot be recovered. It is similar to the safe format option in the Norton Utilities - use with care!

MIRROR, UNDELETE, UNFORMAT

It is now possible with MS-DOS 5.0 to recover files and information on disks through the use of the UNDELETE and UNFORMAT commands. When the MIRROR program is loaded it maintains a catalogue of all disk activity and this is used when you want to undelete a file.

The UNDELETE command will still work even if the MIRROR program has not been loaded. In this event a search is made of the MS-DOS file allocation table (FAT) and you are prompted for the missing first letter from the filename of the deleted file.

The UNFORMAT command will only work on disks which have NOT been reformatted with the unconditional switch (/U) on the FORMAT command.

SETVER

Some applications check to see which version of MS-DOS is running before they begin executing. MS-DOS 5.0 reports a different version number and this can cause problems. To get around this problem, a utility is supplied with MS-DOS 5.0 which contains a list of EXE files and the DOS version numbers that should be reported to them.

The SETVER list can be added to as the need arises. As with most of the utility programs supplied with MS-DOS 5.0 it can be loaded above 640K if there is sufficient free space.

MS-DOS 5.0 Shell

The shell supplied with MS-DOS 5.0 is completely new, with many of its features being 'borrowed' from Windows 3.

As can be seen in figure 6.13 the screen is divided up into four sections; directory tree, file list, program groups and the active task list. The first two are self explanatory, the second two however are worth further discussion.

As with Windows 3, applications of a similar nature can be assembled into what are called Program Groups. Each application within a group needs to have certain system settings defined; these settings are similar to those found in the Windows 3 program information files (PIF). For readers who are unfamiliar with Windows 3 these settings cover such things as program name, description, start-up directory and conventional memory requirements.

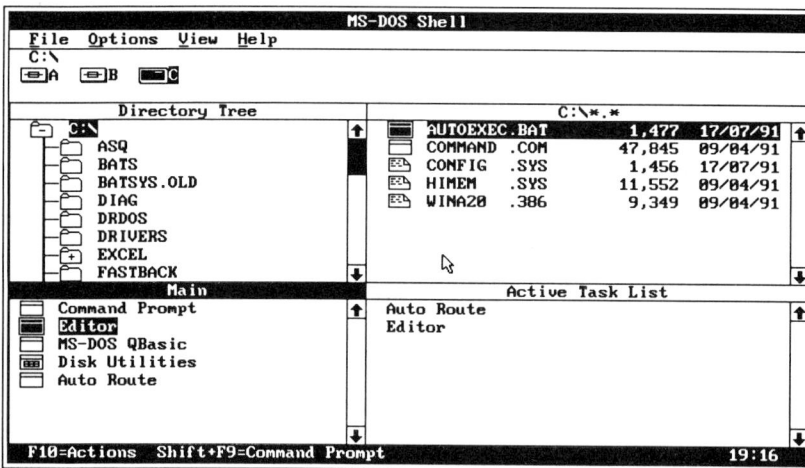

```
                              MS-DOS Shell
   File  Options  View  Help
   C:\
   [=]A    [=]B   [==]C

        Directory Tree                      C:\*.*
   [-] C:\                    ↑   [■] AUTOEXEC.BAT    1,477  17/07/91  ↑
      [=] ASQ                     [ ] COMMAND  .COM  47,845  09/04/91
      [=] BATS                    [=] CONFIG   .SYS   1,456  17/07/91
      [=] BATSYS.OLD              [=] HIMEM    .SYS  11,552  09/04/91
      [=] DIAG                    [=] WINA20   .386   9,349  09/04/91
      [=] DRDOS
      [=] DRIVERS
      [+] EXCEL                          ↳
      [=] FASTBACK            ↓                                      ↓
            Main                          Active Task List
   [ ] Command Prompt         ↑   Auto Route                        ↑
   [■] Editor                     Editor
   [ ] MS-DOS QBasic
   [▦] Disk Utilities
   [ ] Auto Route

                              ↓                                     ↓
   F10=Actions  Shift+F9=Command Prompt                    19:16
```

Figure 6.13 MS-DOS 5.0 shell.

The task list is the most exciting new feature of the shell. Microsoft has added a task switching facility which allows more than one program to be run simultaneously. It is important to realise that the non-active applications are in a suspended state, i.e. they are NOT executing in the background.

The method employed to switch between tasks is similar to that of Windows 3 when running in Real and Standard mode. This method of task switching means it is inadvisable to switch any programs that need to be active all the time, e.g. communication programs such as 3270 emulation or networks.

In the MS-DOS 5.0 directory on your hard disk you will find a file called DOSSHELL.INI. If you edit the file with the MS-DOS editor you will see it contains a number of settings including the names of the program groups and the colour definitions. If you want to create your own custom colours for the shell (a facility lacking in the current version) copy one of the colour definitions using the block copy command, alter the title and set the screen elements to the colours you want. The next time you load the shell and select COLOURS from the OPTIONS pull-down menu your settings should be amongst those listed.

N.B. **Before attempting to edit the DOSSHELL.INI file it is recommended that you make a backup copy of it.**

Microsoft Quick BASIC

For users of GW-BASIC, Microsoft has included a new version of BASIC with MS-DOS 5.0 called Quick BASIC. This is an interpreted version of the popular Quick BASIC compiler.

Old GW-BASIC programs can be converted and run by using the REMLINE.BAS program in the DOS directory. This will read GW-BASIC source code (pre-saved with ',A' option) and remove the line numbers.

Improvements over GW-BASIC are improved execution speed, full screen editor and online help. Also programs developed in Quick

BASIC can be compiled with the Quick BASIC compiler as the two applications are language compatible.

Large Partition and Floppy Disk Support

In response to the increasing size of hard disks, MS-DOS 5.0 can support partitions of up to 2GB. The need to install the SHARE program for partitions larger than 32MB, as with MS-DOS 4.01, has been removed which means further memory savings.

The SHARE program only needs to be active if you are running in a multi-tasking environment such as Windows 3 or accessing a network. If there is sufficient upper memory available the LOADHIGH command can be used to load the SHARE utility above the 640K line.

The other improvement to MS-DOS 5.0 disk management facilities is the support for the new 3.5" double sided/high density (2.88MB) floppy disk drives. The number of PCs with this type of drive fitted will increase and it is likely to become the new floppy disk standard. For backward compatibility MS-DOS 5.0 also supports disk sizes from 160K (5.25" single sided/double density) through to 1.44MB (3.5" double sided/quad density).

FILES SYSTEMS FUTURE

In an operating system, it is the file systems job to manage file input and output and to control the format of information on any storage media. MS-DOS has always (only) used the File Allocation Table, commonly known as FAT as its file system. FAT was originally designed in 1977 by Bill Gates and Marc McDonald for (and around) 800K floppy disks.

With FAT, each logical volume, which can be a floppy disk or hard drive, has its own File Allocation Table. FAT serves two functions: it contains the allocation information for each file on the volume (in the form of linked lists of allocation units) and it indicates which allocation units are free for assignment to a file that is being created or extended.

As we all know, FAT is limited by the naming convention of an eight character file name followed by a three character extension. This is very cumbersome and FAT, when used with large hard disks, can be very slow.

For compatibility reasons, FAT will always be with us. However we may see something that has been called, in the OS/2 world at least, SuperFAT. IBM when building the 32-bit version of OS/2 (version 2.0) completely re-wrote the DOS File Allocation Table. By doing so, they took full advantage of their new 32-bit operating system (and the Intel range of 32-bit microprocessors it runs on) to build a very fast file system whilst retaining complete backward compatibility with the existing FAT. This improved FAT is one of the reasons why you might see statistics, that DOS applications executing under OS/2 normally run much faster than DOS applications running under DOS.

It is not unlikely that Microsoft will use the same technology (or even the same code) and produce a SuperFAT type of file system for those DOS users using a PC with a 32-bit CPU.

Installable File Systems

Future versions of MS-DOS will include Installable File Systems (IFS). When Microsoft and IBM were jointly designing OS/2 it was realised early on that as disk drive (and other) technology evolved, new software file systems would be needed to obtain the best performance from them as a single built-in file system would not easily be able to accommodate all possible devices.

You will find that with the uptake of installable file systems, the door will be opened to rapid file system evolution and innovation. Storage media manufacturers and third party suppliers will build and supply their own unique file systems that make optimum use of their drive technology. Installable file systems will therefore make it possible for MS-DOS to access multiple incompatible volume structures; FAT (as at present), HPFS (High Performance File System) - which is dealt with later - and probably other media such as CD-ROM, WORM (Write Once Read Many) drives and perhaps even UNIX volumes.

New Technology File System (NTFS)

The High Performance File System (HPFS) was designed by Microsoft's Gordon Letwin (the chief architect of OS/2) and was originally conceived for Microsoft's network division. Under OS/2, the HPFS is an example of an optional Installable File System (IFS).

HPFS has been renamed to NTFS by Microsoft and will probably be introduced as an IFS to both MS-DOS and NT versions of Windows.

HPFS was designed to provide extremely fast access to very large disk volumes e.g. servers. Features of HPFS that make it very attractive as a file system are:

o   File names up to 254 characters in length.
o   Fast access to very large disk volumes.
o   Strategic allocation of directory structures.
o   Caching of directories, data and file system structures.
o   Large file support.

To give you some ideas as to what to expect, we describe the HPFS seen with versions of OS/2 at present.

To increase performance, HPFS uses advanced data structures (such as B-trees and B+trees), contiguous sector allocation, intelligent caching, read-ahead and deferred writes and can handle individual file sizes of up to 2 Gigabytes.

The B-trees and B+trees allow fast random access to filenames, directory names, lists of sectors allocated to file or directories and to simple data structures for locating chunks of free space the appropriate size. The routines that manipulate these data structures are written in assembly language and will have been carefully tuned to give the best performance.

To save the disk's read/write head from having to move from one track to another when accessing files, HPFS will assign consecutive sectors to files whenever possible - thus minimising head movement. HPFS also keeps control structures (things called Fnodes and free space bitmaps) near the data structures that they control.

To keep files from being fragmented HPFS tries to scatter newly created files across the disk. This is so that the sectors allocated to the files as they are extended will not be interleaved.

The HPFS has its own specialised cache program (separate from other cache features, and is normally invoked automatically when a user requests a primary HPFS partition. HPFS caches sectors (as does the FAT file system) but unlike the FAT file system, HPFS can manage very large caches efficiently and adjusts sector caching on a per-handle basis depending on which manner the file is used. HPFS also caches pathnames and directories and transforms disk directory entries into a very compact and memory-efficient representation. Like most caches, HPFS also pre-reads data that it believes a program or application is likely to need. Whenever a program issues relatively small read requests, the file system always fetches data from the file in 2KB chunks and caches the excess, allowing later read operations to be satisfied from the cache.

FUTURE VERSIONS OF MS-DOS

Over the next few years we will definitely be seeing 5.x and 6.0 versions of MS-DOS. Microsoft as we mentioned earlier are fully committed to improving and enhancing MS-DOS and will be including the improved and new file systems that we have just discussed.

We will definitely be seeing MS-DOS made more configurable to the PC it is being installed or run on. This will take the shape of self-configuration, similar to that found with Windows 3.x today. MS-DOS will detect and modify itself depending on whether the machine contains an 8088/8086, 80286 or more likely an i386 or i486 Microprocessor. Each mode will be able to take full advantage of the microprocessor it runs on, particularly of course with the powerful Intel 32-bit microprocessors, and there will be much more synergy with Windows.

The way Personal Computers are being used in more and more businesses will directly affect what is added into future MS-DOS releases. You will therefore find that MS-DOS has additions and enhancements that make it much more 'Network Friendly'. For network system vendors and network administrators this will be of real benefit.

We look forward to having our 'old friend' DOS continuously revised and improved and with us over the next decade.

CHAPTER

7

MEMORY MANAGEMENT

Windows comes with its own memory management software (HIMEM.SYS and EMM386.SYS). These can conflict with older versions of third-party memory management software packages such as 386MAX and QEMM.

Newer versions and upgrades of 386MAX and QEMM have been released, which support Windows in all three modes. If you are currently using the older versions of 386MAX or QEMM and have trouble in using them with Windows contact, the manufacturers to get an upgrade.

Note also that the versions of HIMEM.SYS and EMM386.EXE supplied with MS-DOS 5.0 supersede those issued with Windows. MS-DOS 5.0 offers a whole host of benefits over previous versions of DOS (and in some simple cases negates the need for the user to add memory management software) - this has already been described in Chapter 6.

In many cases however, whilst using Windows, you will still find that large memory-intensive applications may not have sufficient conventional memory in which to run. If this is the case, you will need to relocate TSRs, device and network drivers using a third party memory management package that supports Windows.

RUNNING OUT OF MEMORY?

When running applications under Windows you may receive a
message informing you that there is insufficient memory. It is
possible to find out the type and amount of memory available by
clicking on the ABOUT option on the HELP menu in either the
PROGRAM MANAGER or FILE MANAGER. The resulting screen
is shown in figure 7.1.

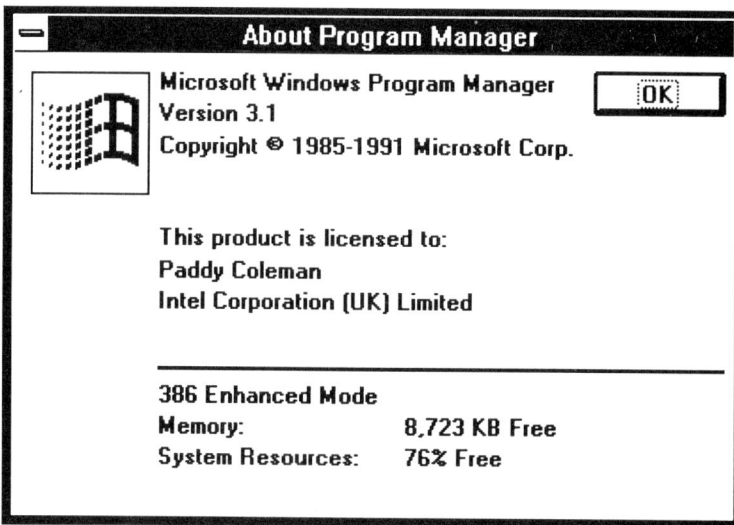

```
┌─────────────────────────────────────────────────────┐
│ ▬         About Program Manager                       │
├─────────────────────────────────────────────────────┤
│        Microsoft Windows Program Manager    ┌──────┐  │
│  [▦]   Version 3.1                          │  OK  │  │
│        Copyright © 1985-1991 Microsoft Corp. └──────┘  │
│                                                       │
│        This product is licensed to:                   │
│        Paddy Coleman                                  │
│        Intel Corporation (UK) Limited                 │
│        ─────────────────────────────────────         │
│        386 Enhanced Mode                              │
│        Memory:              8.723 KB Free             │
│        System Resources:    76% Free                  │
└─────────────────────────────────────────────────────┘
```

Figure 7.1 About box displayed from the PROGRAM or FILE MANAGERS.

The figures reported in the ABOUT box differ depending on the
mode Windows is running in and also on what type of memory is
installed in your PC. The following explains how the figures are
calculated and where possible suggests how to increase the memory
available.

If you are unsure about all the different types of PC memory,
Appendix B gives a detailed explanation of each type.

Amount of Memory Free

This number is the amount of memory currently available for applications. When you run Windows in Standard mode, this number will include extended memory. When you run Windows in 386 Enhanced mode, this number will include virtual memory and could be much larger than the physical amount of memory installed in your computer.

If you need more memory or if the amount of free memory is less than 30K, close some applications. Check the Program Information Files of any MS-DOS applications to ensure that memory is not being allocated to them that they do not need. For example, the 3270 emulation software provided with VINES only requires 256K of conventional memory to run and so a setting of 640K in the PIF is wasteful. Many applications do not necessarily utilise expanded (EMS) and/or extended (XMS) memory. The settings for EMS and XMS in the PIF can therefore be set to zero, thus reducing an applications demand on the available resources.

Amount of Expanded Memory (EMS) Free

When you run Windows in Real mode with an expanded memory driver installed, this number shows the amount of expanded memory currently available. It is possible to have plenty of expanded memory available, but be out of conventional memory.

You can close some applications to free up conventional memory. Many users' AUTOEXEC.BAT and CONFIG.SYS files contain device drivers and TSRs that are not strictly needed and waste valuable conventional memory. Figure 7.2 shows the minimum AUTOEXEC.BAT and CONFIG.SYS files required for Windows and can be used as a basis for streamlining your own.

```
PATH C:\DOS;C:\WINDOWS
PROMPT $P$G
SET COMSPEC=C:\DOS\COMMAND.COM
SET TEMP=C:\WINDOWS\TEMP
KEYB UK,,C:\DOS\KEYBOARD.SYS

SHELL=C:\COMMAND.COM C:\ /P /E:2048
COUNTRY=044,,C:\DOS\COUNTRY.SYS
DEVICE=C:\HIMEM.SYS
DEVICE=C:\DOS\SMARTDRV.SYS 1024 0
FILES=30
BUFFERS=1,1
STACKS=0,0
LASTDRIVE=C
```

Figure 7.2 Minimum AUTOEXEC.BAT and CONFIG.SYS files for Windows.

Smartdrive Amount

This number shows the amount of extended memory that is currently being used by the Windows disk cache utility, SMARTDRIVE. Windows can shrink and grow the size of the disk cache according to memory requirements.

SMARTDRIVE is installed for use with Windows by adding the following line to your CONFIG.SYS file:

```
DEVICE=C:\WINDOWS\SMARTDRV.SYS xxxx yyyy
```

The xxxx parameter specifies the desired size of the disk cache, and the yyyy parameter the minimum that it can be reduced to by Windows. If you are really short on memory you may wish to set the Minimum Cache Setting to zero (this is the option shown in figure 7.2).

The caching method employed by SMARTDRIVE is discussed at length in Chapter 10.

System Resources

System Resources are two 64K buffers whose size cannot be changed by the user. They are responsible for any graphical display and driver used by Windows.

The number in the dialog box is the percentage of System Resources available (it will never reach 100% because the system itself takes up some). If this number is too low (about 10%), you cannot run any more applications regardless of how much free memory you have. Also it is possible (and common) to receive out of memory errors yet have plenty of available memory free.

Once the System Resources are filled, the only way to free them is to close applications. A problem in Windows version 3.0 is that the opening of Program Manager groups uses up valuable System Resources and there is no way to reclaim this memory apart from closing all your applications and restarting Windows. This has been rectified and is not the case with Windows version 3.1.

EXTENDED MEMORY MANAGER (HIMEM.SYS)

HIMEM.SYS is a driver required by Windows for managing extended memory. It must be included in your CONFIG.SYS file. The method HIMEM uses to access extended memory depends on your hardware.

Once HIMEM has loaded, you will see a message similar to the following informing you of the method HIMEM will use to access extended memory on your computer:

```
Installed A20 handler number X.
```

where X is a value of 1 through 8 which corresponds to one of the methods in the table in figure 7.3.

NUMBER	NAME	COMPUTER TYPE
1	AT	IBM AT or 100% compatible
2	PS/2	IBM PS/2
3	PTLCASCADE	Phoenix Cascade BIOS
4	HPVECTRA	HP Vectra (A & A+)
5	ATT6300PLUS	AT&T 6300 Plus
6	ACER1100	Acer 1100
7	Toshiba	Toshiba 1200XE and 1600
8	Wyse	Wyse 12.5Mhz 80286

Figure 7.3 (Windows) HIMEM method of accessing extended memory

If HIMEM does not work properly, you can try a different method: specify the switch for your computer type on the DEVICE=HIMEM.SYS line in your CONFIG.SYS file. Computer type corresponds to either the number or the name of your computer from the table. For example, the following lines are equivalent:

```
DEVICE=C:\HIMEM.SYS /M:PS2
DEVICE=C:\HIMEM.SYS /M:2
```

Either of these entries will force HIMEM to use the IBM PS/2 A20 method for accessing extended memory. Note that the HIMEM.SYS supplied with MS-DOS 5.0 has more allowable entries - this is explained further in Chapter 6.

EXPANDED MEMORY EMULATOR (EMM386.SYS)

The EMM386.SYS driver supplied with Windows is used on computers equipped with an Intel386 or Intel486 microprocessor to simulate expanded memory using extended memory.

With versions of MS-DOS earlier than release 5.0 the EMM386.SYS driver is optional and only needs to be installed if you require the use of expanded memory with MS-DOS applications OUTSIDE of Windows. Expanded memory can be made available to MS-DOS applications running under the control of Windows via the EMS parameter in the PIF settings.

The new version of EMM386 supplied with MS-DOS 5.0 is used to optionally provide expanded memory to applications inside and outside of Windows and also to manage the upper memory area. This added level of complexity means it is no longer possible to provide expanded memory inside Windows via the PIF settings unless EMM386 has been installed.

SWAPFILE

SWAPFILE is a utility which can be used to dramatically increase the performance of Windows when running in 386 Enhanced mode. SWAPFILE turns a contiguous portion of hard disk into additional memory which Windows can access (very quickly as it is permanently allocated).

SWAPFILE cannot be used with all hard disk drives due to the way some drives interact with MS-DOS (if the drive formatted with MS-DOS FDISK/FORMAT combination, all will be well).

There is a different procedure to create a SWAPFILE between version 3.0 and 3.1 of Windows, the latter being the easier.

To create a permanent SWAPFILE for Windows 3.0 do the following:

(1) Start Windows in Real mode (WIN /R).

(2) Close down any applications that run automatically.

(3) Click on the RUN option in the FILE MANAGER and enter SWAPFILE.EXE in the command line box.

(4) If a permanent swapfile already exists you will be asked if you wish to delete it and create a new one, just delete it or cancel the operation.

(5) A dialog box is displayed showing the maximum and minimum possible sizes for your swapfile. From these figures Windows suggests a reasonable size which you are able to alter.

(6) Click on the CREATE button and the swapfile will be created.

With Windows 3.1 creating a permanent SWAPFILE is a simple matter of selecting the 386 Enhanced option from the CONTROL PANEL. This is shown in figure 7.4.

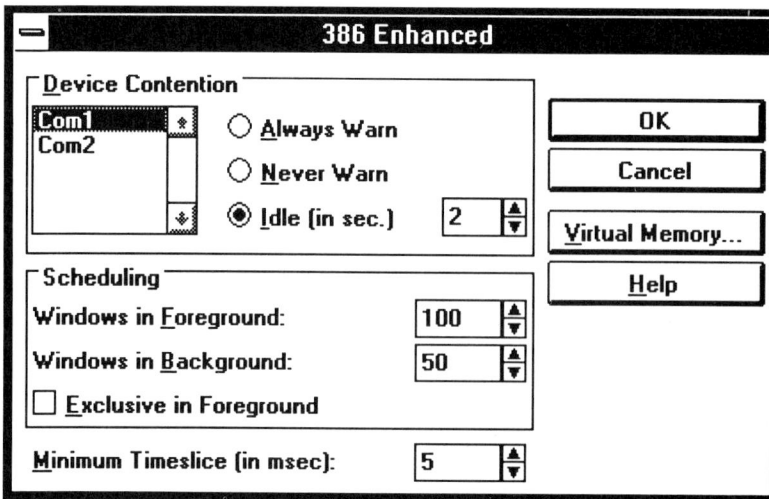

Figure 7.4 386 Enhanced Control Panel option for Windows 3.1.

Choosing the VIRTUAL MEMORY option from the 386 Enhanced dialog box gives a further dialog box as shown in figure 7.5.

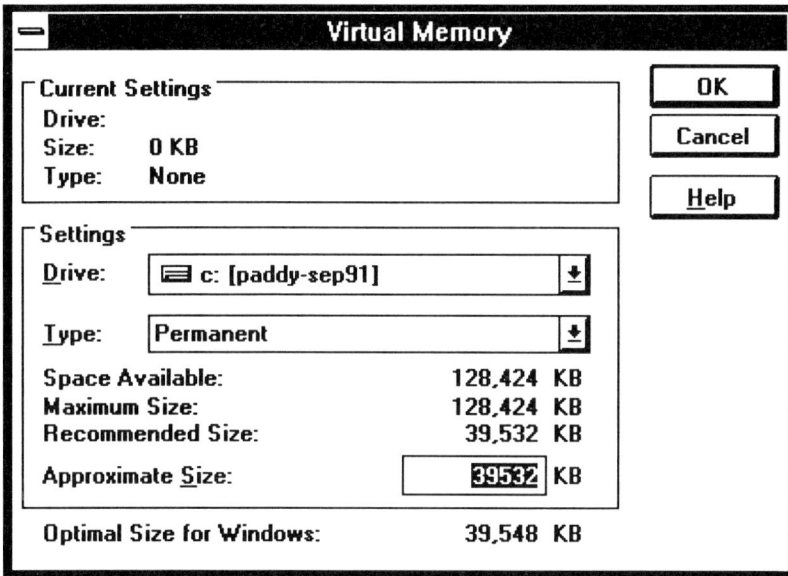

Figure 7.5 Building a permanent SWAPFILE in Windows 3.1.

You can either select the recommended size or enter a value up to four times the amount of your physical system memory, e.g. for a four megabyte machine enter a value of not more than sixteen megabytes.

In order for Windows to be able to create a permanent swapfile your hard disk must have a large amount of contiguous free space. If you have never compacted your hard disk you will need to do this first. Norton Utilities has a program called Norton Speed Disk which can compact the files on your hard disk.

386 ENHANCED MODE SWAPPING

Windows (running in 386 Enhanced mode) will not provide virtual memory support with a temporary swap file unless there is a minimum of 1.5MB of hard disk space free on the paging drive. If Windows is not swapping due to low disk space, you must either free up space on the drive or change paging drives (if another one is available). SYSTEM.INI contains the setting:

```
PagingDrive=<drive-letter>
```

The purpose of this setting is to specify the disk drive where Windows (in 386 Enhanced mode) will allocate a temporary swap file.

The setting is ignored if you have set up a permanent swap file. If you do not have a permanent swap file and no drive is specified, or the specified drive does not exist, Windows will attempt to put your temporary swap file on the drive containing the SYSTEM.INI file. If all the possible drives (explicit and implicit) are full then paging will be disabled.

386MAX 5.1 FROM QUALITAS

Qualitas 386MAX memory management products run on any personal computer equipped with either an Intel386 or Intel486 microprocessor with 256K extended memory running MS-DOS 3.0 or later.

They are designed to provide the maximum possible memory to MS-DOS applications by moving device drivers and terminate and stay resident programs (TSRs) out of conventional memory (the lower 640KB) and to provide memory support services to those programs that can use memory beyond 640KB through one of the current memory specifications (such as LIM EMS).

Early versions of 386MAX (before version 5.0) are incompatible with Windows' own memory management software. 386MAX 5.0 provided support to Windows users running in Real mode.

386MAX 5.1 is fully compatible with Windows (in Real or 386 Enhanced mode) and is what we will discuss here (note that registered users of 386MAX 5.0 should have received upgrades to 386MAX 5.1 free of charge).

If you have any earlier version than 5.0, then we suggest you upgrade or purchase 386MAX 5.1 as soon as possible - in our opinion it is the best memory management software around at the moment.

386MAX 5.1 when operating under Windows, replaces the Microsoft supplied HIMEM.SYS extended memory manager and provides much more functionality (as well as occupying only 1K of conventional memory - one third of what HIMEM.SYS requires). 386MAX 5.1 also supports a technique called instancing, that allows resident programs (such as Borland's Sidekick) to run simultaneously and can be loaded into either conventional or high MS-DOS memory before starting Windows.

Getting an optimum configuration with any PC, different memory amounts, miscellaneous device drivers, differing display adaptors, network cards etc. can be an incredibly difficult process and there are often few guidelines to go by. 386MAX 5.x comes with a MAXIMIZE utility that automatically configures available memory and optimises your system for use with 386MAX.

This process is amazing and cannot be flawed. The entire MAXIMIZE process only takes a few minutes, defaults can be overridden if necessary and the MAXIMIZE process can be run any time after installation - for example if you were to make a change to your configuration.

The 386MAX documentation covers most of the things you need to know and there is no point in covering them here. The only things that we would add are:

(1) Always keep up to date with the various releases of 386MAX that come out. Install different versions of 386MAX in separate directories in case you wish to fall back to a previous release.

   As an example we originally installed 386MAX 5.0 in a sub-directory on our hard drive called:

   ```
   C:\386MAX50
   ```

   Whilst testing out 386MAX 5.1 we installed it in another sub-directory called:

   ```
   C:\386MAX51
   ```

(2) To make your life easier always use the PROFILE technique when specifying options to the 386MAX device driver.

   For example in your CONFIG.SYS you will have the line:

   ```
   DEVICE=C:\386MAX51\386MAX.SYS      PRO=C:\386MAX51\386MAX.PRO
   ```

   and in your 386MAX working sub-directory (C:\386MAX51 in this case) you will have the 386MAX.PRO text file which may look like:

   ```
   ;
   ; 386MAX 5.1 installed on Toshiba T5200 (8MB RAM)
   ;
   ; Author : Adrian Jonathan Cotterill
   ```

```
; Date    : 3rd August 1991
;
VGA            ; Protect VGA video area
RAM=C800-CC00 ; Protect network card BIOS location
;
; Following line adds 32KB to high DOS
;
USE=B000-B800
;
```

As you can see, this allows you to list your options as one per line, add comments and give reasons as to why you have specified that option.

Although 386MAX 5.1 will work with IBM PS/2s the results will be somewhat disappointing. BlueMAX also by Qualitas is very similar to 386MAX but has been tailored to the quirks of the IBM PS/2. BlueMAX is discussed later in this chapter.

Automatic Instancing

386MAX's Windows support includes a proprietary feature called 'Automatic Instancing'. This feature allows many programs that are not Windows-aware to work properly with Windows. TSRs and device drivers that are not Windows-aware may not function correctly when in Windows. This is the case for many TSRs and device drivers currently available (you should refer to the Windows User's Guide for more information on this problem.)

If you have encountered resident programs that have not functioned properly with Windows or needed to be loaded in an open MS-DOS window, 386MAX should allow them to work properly. If programs still do not function correctly, Qualitas Technical Support should be able to resolve the difficulty.

For More Conventional Memory

Windows is able to take advantage of unused linear address space between 640KB and 1MB to reduce its own memory overhead in low

DOS. If Windows detects the presence of unused linear address space in high DOS at startup, it will map the addresses with physical RAM and load a small portion of its data into the re-mapped RAM. Because 386MAX may be mapping all the unused high DOS address space before Windows is loaded, you must be sure to leave some space unmapped to take advantage of this feature.

If INSTALL/UPDATE detects an available monochrome display area it will map only the first 8KB of the available space by inserting appropriate USE statements in the options profile. By doing so, Windows will take advantage of a portion of the remaining space.
Although Windows will make use of a portion of the unmapped space, it may not always be the most effective use of the space on all systems. This is a result of the fact that the unmapped space could have been mapped as high DOS by 386MAX and used to store resident software which may be forced to reside in conventional memory.

If you have already installed 386MAX and have recovered the monochrome display area with a USE statement in the B000-B800 range, we suggest you open a MS-DOS window and display the 386UTIL MAPMEM screen to determine the amount of conventional memory available. Then, change the USE statement to read USE=B000-B200, re-boot the system and rerun MAXIMIZE. After MAXIMIZE has completed, restart Windows and again display the 386UTIL MAPMEM screen in a MS-DOS window. Finally, compare the amount of conventional memory available before and after to determine which setting is optimal for your system.

For 386 Enhanced Compatibility

386MAX.VxD (the Windows Virtual Device) must be in the same subdirectory as 386MAX.SYS for compatibility in Windows 386 Enhanced mode.

Also, in order to provide support for Windows in 386 Enhanced mode, 386MAX.SYS conventional memory storage size has increased from 80 to 1104 bytes - obiously quite significant! If you do not require Windows 3.x Enhanced mode support, you should add a NOWIN3 statement to the 386MAX.SYS options profile. Using this option allows Windows 3.0 use in Real mode only.

Trouble-shooting

386MAX.SYS and 386MAX.VxD must pass memory parameters to Windows when Windows attempts to initialise in 386 Enhanced mode. Once Windows has completed initialisation, 386MAX.SYS is switched to OFF mode and the involvement of 386MAX.VxD is minimal. Therefore, it is unlikely that problems encountered while running Windows in Enhanced mode are a result of 386MAX support.

Windows will start up with a different set of initialisation parameters with 386MAX in the system than without. This may result in problems that appear only when 386MAX is in the system but are not 386MAX problems. The following outlines a process that will aid while attempting to isolate the source of a problem.

Comment the DEVICE=386MAX.SYS line in CONFIG.SYS and any references to 386LOAD in CONFIG.SYS or AUTOEXEC.BAT.

Load all device drivers and TSRs into low memory.

Add the following two DEVICE= statements, in the order listed, to CONFIG.SYS:

```
DEVICE=C:\HIMEM.SYS
DEVICE=C:\WINDOWS\EMM386.SYS
```

Note that the path statements used above may differ on your system. Also, to simplify the process in the future, do not remove edited lines but simply remark them so they can be reused easily.

After making the above changes in CONFIG.SYS, re-boot the system and attempt to reproduce the problem. If the problem still exists and you require further assistance, be sure to notify any support representative (Qualitas, Microsoft or the application manufacturer's) of the results of the above test. The results do not completely implicate nor absolve any parties involved, but the information is useful. Performing this step will speed up the technical support process.

SYSTEM.INI Options

There are potential conflicts with Windows when the address space normally occupied by the system ROM is re-mapped. Because memory managers frequently re-map system ROM address space, the following statement must be added to the [386Enh] section of SYSTEM.INI:

```
SystemROMBreakPoint=FALSE
```

Programs that require VCPI to enter protected mode do not work under Windows. By default, all VCPI requests cause Windows to terminate the application. Windows can be made to return an error and the application can continue to load without using VCPI calls by adding the following line to the [386Enh] section of SYSTEM.INI:

```
VCPIWarning=FALSE
```

BLUEMAX FOR PS/2S

Few people are aware that there is a subtle hardware difference between IBM PS/2s and other MS-DOS computers. In a PS/2 the

ROM (read only memory) which holds the BIOS (basic input output system) is 128KB, double the size of most other MS-DOS personal computers. This ROM BIOS (like in other computers) is located at the top of MS-DOS' first megabyte, well out of the first 640KB where applications actually reside. You will not feel the cost of the 128KB BIOS unless you are running PC-DOS and wish to run a 386 memory management routine to load utilities and device drivers into the free address space between 640KB and 1MB. If you do, you do not have so much room to play with.

BlueMAX from Qualitas, Inc. is a 386 memory manager specifically designed for IBM's PS/2 range of personal computers. By compressing unnecessary information out of this 128KB system BIOS, BlueMAX is able to recover 80-84KB contiguous RAM. In many systems this amounts to a 65% gain in high DOS memory.

An example should illustrate the basic premise of BlueMAX that not all of the instructions in the BIOS are needed for normal use.

First of all, the PS/2 was designed with OS/2 in mind. The PS/2 includes additional software routines, known as the A-BIOS, in the 128KB BIOS. If you are using DOS these routines have no value.

Power-on self test (POST) routines are instructions which verify that the PS/2 is working when first turned on. These are accessed only once each time the computer is turned on.

IBM (and other manufacturers) supply a rarely used BASIC programming interpreter into the BIOS which can be harmlessly compressed out. ROMs always come in fixed sizes and there is usually space left over after all the software has been written to the BIOS by the manufacturer. This is true of the PS/2, and this valuable memory which lies untouched can be used by BlueMAX.

BlueMAX includes all the features found in 386MAX 5.x. If you are running Windows (and PC-DOS) on an IBM PS/2 and need to use memory management software, then you should be using BlueMAX.

QUALITAS STRIP MANAGER

STRIPMGR is a program supplied with and for use with Qualitas 386MAX. It scans CONFIG.SYS, AUTOEXEC.BAT, and any batch files called by AUTOEXEC, and optionally removes 386 memory managers and their related programs. STRIPMGR returns the number of memory managers and programs found or removed (depending on various switches), or 255 on an error.

The syntax is:

```
STRIPMGR [d:] [/H/S/T] [~386MAX.SYS] [striplist]
```

The switches are:

/H   Display the help screen.

/S   Strip the memory managers. STRIPMGR will prompt the user before removing each program, unless the /T switch is specified (see below). If the /S switch is not specified, STRIPMGR will display the files found but take no action.

/T   Terse mode - turn off the display of STRIPMGR's processing, and if /S is specified, remove the programs without prompting the user.

The optional arguments are:

d: Startup drive (where CONFIG.SYS and
                        AUTOEXEC.BAT are located).

~386MAX.SYS   Do not remove references to 386MAX or any
                        of its associated programs. (Note that the name
                        could be changed, i.e. ~QEMM.SYS to not
                        remove any references to QEMM.)

striplist   The name of the strip list file. If not specified,
                        it defaults to STRIPMGR.LST in the same
                        directory as STRIPMGR.

The format of the strip list is:

```
: QEMM 386 from Quarterdeck
QEMM.SYS
~LOADHI
!NOEGA

: 386MAX from Qualitas
386MAX.SYS
~386LOAD *PROG=
```

Lines beginning with a colon (:) or semi-colon (;) are comments and
are ignored, as are blank lines. A program name in the left column
is the memory manager name; it is followed by the names of its
associated programs with leading tabs. If STRIPMGR matches the
memory manager name with a name in CONFIG.SYS, it saves the
associated programs to a 'delete list' and scans CONFIG.SYS and
AUTOEXEC (and related batch files) for a match. Otherwise, the
associated programs are ignored.

The associated programs have required leading characters:

!   Remove the entire line where the program name
                           specified occurs.

~   Remove the program name and any switches (/
                           or -) which follow, but keep the remainder of
                           the line.

If the associated program has a ~, it can also take optional
arguments.

```
~386load GETSIZE RAM NOVID
```

will remove any matching arguments (GETSIZE, RAM, NOVID)
from the line. If the argument is preceded by an asterisk (*), it is
assumed to be the last valid argument on the line, and everything is
removed up to and including that argument:

```
~386load *prog=
```

CHAPTER

8

WINDOWS APPLICATIONS

This chapter describes a number of Windows applications, some of the problems you may encounter when running them and various hints and tips for each application. At the end of this chapter we discuss Microsoft's Object Linking and Embedding protocols.

ADOBE TYPE MANAGER

Adobe Type Manager (ATM) is a software package that eliminates jagged fonts in almost any Windows application, whether it be a word-processing, page-layout, spreadsheet or graphics program. To use ATM you need a PC with an 80286 or above processor and at least one megabyte of memory (although 2MB is recommended).

Once the ATM software is installed, it will work under Windows automatically allowing your screen to display high-quality typefaces of any size or style. ATM incorporates Postscript outline font technology that also enables inexpensive printers to print Postscript language fonts that are crisp and smooth.

Figure 8.1 shows the letter (A) reproduced here at 80 Dots Per Inch (DPI) in Windows WRITE using a Times Roman font with ATM switched on.

Figure 8.1 Times Roman 80 DPI, ATM on.

Figure 8.2 shows the letter (A) reproduced at 80 Dots Per Inch (DPI), again in Windows WRITE using a Times Roman font with ATM switched off.

Figure 8.2 Times Roman 80 DPI, ATM off.

Note that figure 8.1 looks much crisper and neater than figure 8.2.

The ATM package includes the outlines fonts that you need to display and print high-quality type in various sizes and styles for the Times, Helvetica, Courier and Symbol typefaces. Other fonts can be bought to add to this collection. ATM is compatible with any non-copy protected Postscript language Type 1 format font software, including the Adobe Type library fonts and Type 1 software packages from other vendors.

A font cache is available via the ATM control panel, see figure 8.3. This allows you to determine the amount of system memory available to store font information.

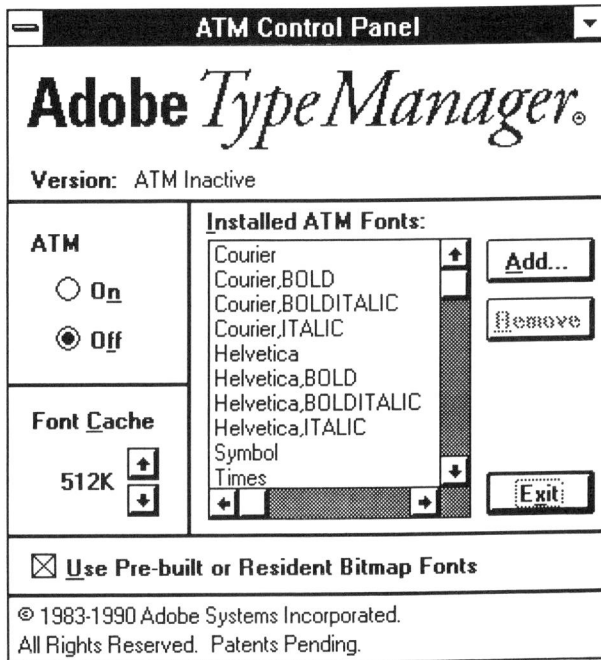

Figure 8.3 ATM Control Panel.

The default setting for the font cache is 96K, although depending on the amount of memory you have available in your system you can set the font cache from 64K to 8192K. To improve performance you may want to increase the font cache size parameter and see how it affects your applications. For example, if your applications seem unusually slow when you scroll, change pages or display fonts, your font cache is probably too small. However, do be careful with the font cache setting. If you set ATM's font cache to be larger than the amount of memory available on your PC, you may not be able to run the ATM Control Panel. If this happens, quit Windows and use a DOS editor to delete the line 'FontCache=xxx' in the ATM.INI file. Then re-start Windows and use the ATM Control Panel to set the font cache to the desired value.

The ATM.INI file contains information on selections made from within Adobe Type Manager. The following sections will appear in ATM.INI:

SECTION	PURPOSE
[Fonts]	Lists the installed fonts.
[Settings]	Defines overall ATM configuration.
[Aliases]	Allows you to substitute one font name for another to ensure compatibility with your existing documents. For example, you can specify that Tms Rmn and Times are the same font.

Windows version 3.1 comes complete with a new outline font technology called TrueType (developed originally by Apple and first implemented in the Macintosh System 7.0 operating system) and now licensed to Microsoft. It is a similar font technology to Adobe Postscript (and hence, also Adobe Type Manager) except that it is not firmly established yet. Microsoft, by including Truetype in Windows itself, are trying to do away with third-party font manager products such as ATM.

If the average Macintosh user's experiences are anything to go by (ATM was originally developed for the Mac before being developed for Windows and then OS/2 Presentation Manager) Windows users will be keeping ATM as it is faster, more powerful and more flexible. However, only time will tell, whether Truetype will become as big a standard as Adobe's Postscript.

Note that a powerful product such as Adobe TypeAlign (an application that lets you place text from any Adobe or other Type 1 font along paths of any angle or shape and then rotate and distort it in order to create a wide variety of special effects) needs ATM in order to work and is probably as good a reason as any for users to buy ATM.

CONTROL PANEL

If you are running Windows 3.0 in Real mode and using expanded memory, a new desktop wallpaper selection will not take effect immediately. You must quit and then restart Windows to see the new selection.

Figure 8.4 Windows version 3.1 CONTROL PANEL.

If your computer does not have copious amounts of memory it is advisable not to install a wallpaper as doing so will decrease the memory available to applications. The CONTROL.INI file contains information from selections made in the Windows CONTROL PANEL. The following sections appear in CONTROL.INI:

```
[Current]
[Color schemes]
[Custom Colors]
[Patterns]
```

The CONTROL.INI file should not be modified by a text editor.

FILE MANAGER

The WINFILE.INI file contains information on and data about selections made from the Windows FILE MANAGER. A typical WINFILE.INI file contains only one section:

```
[Settings]

SaveSettings=1
MinOnRun=0
Replace=0
LowerCase=0
StatusBar=1
CurrentView=0
CurrentSort=201
CurrentAttribs=1841
```

Figure 8.5 Example Windows WINFILE.INI file.

The entries in the WINFILE.INI file must not be edited with a text editor. The FILE MANAGER will update the file when it is terminated. Users should check the value of the setting FileSysChange in their SYSTEM.INI file. This setting indicates to FILE MANAGER whether it should automatically receive messages any time a non-Windows application creates, renames, or deletes a file (in some rare cases this may be of importance). However, if this setting is enabled system performance will be slowed down dramatically. The benefit of the setting being disabled is that it allows a virtual machine to be run exclusively, even when it manipulates files and does not impact system performance.

The major criticism of Windows 3.0 was the poor FILE MANAGER. This has been completely re-written for Windows 3.1 and is shown in figure 8.6. Notice the window layout which is radically different from the version 3.0 FILE MANAGER.

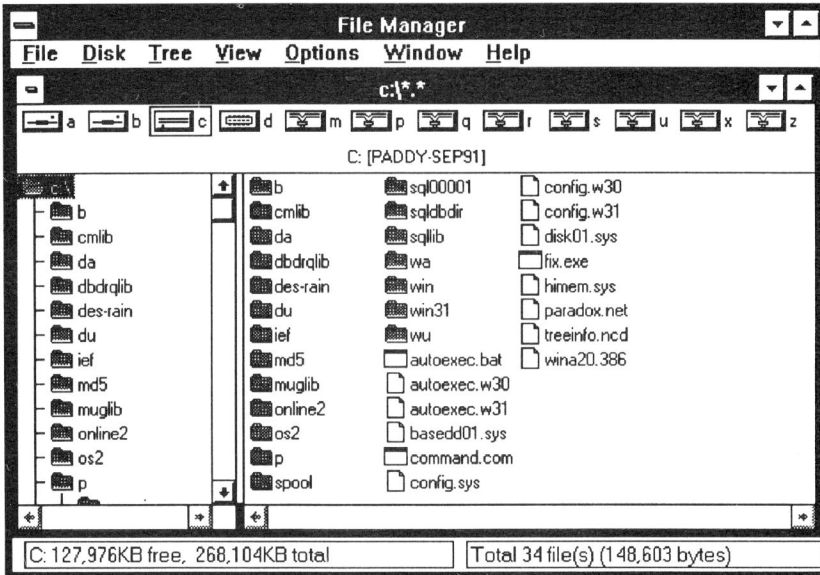

Figure 8.6 The improved FILE MANAGER for Windows version 3.1.

Other major improvements are the much faster performance (especially over networks), improved file association options and a save settings option that actually records worthwhile information!

NOTEPAD

NOTEPAD will support files of almost 64K and no more. There is a problem with the TIME/DATE option of NOTEPAD supplied with Windows version 3.0 since it only enters the date and not the time. This has been fixed in Windows version 3.1.

You can use NOTEPAD to create a log to keep track of how you spend your time. Type in .LOG in capital letters, beginning at the left hand margin of the first line in a NOTEPAD File. From then on, every time you open this file, NOTEPAD will automatically add the current time and date to the end of the file.

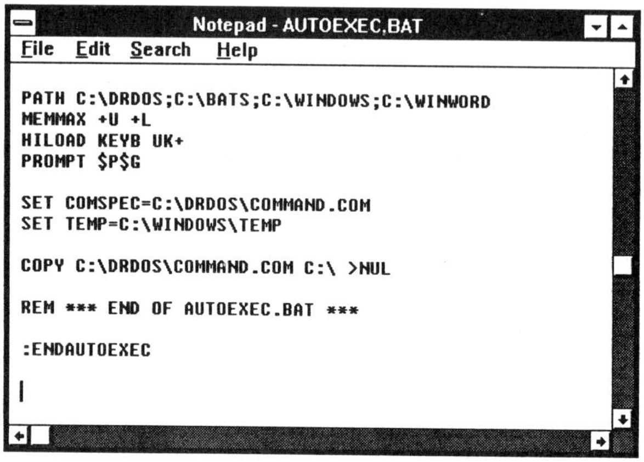

Figure 8.7 Windows NOTEPAD accessory.

Although NOTEPAD lacks the familiar 'search and replace' function found in many editors and word-processors, it is possible to carry out this sort of task with only a minimum of effort. Type your replacement string somewhere in your file, highlight it and then select CUT from the EDIT menu. This transfers your replacement string to the Clipboard. Select SEARCH and then FIND and enter the text you wish to change. Click OK to start searching. When NOTEPAD pauses at the first string found it will highlight the appropriate string. Pressing Del, then Shift-Ins removes the unwanted string and pastes your replacement string from the Clipboard respectively. Searching for further references is a simple case of pressing F3 and continuing the Del, Shift-Ins keyboard sequence.

MS-DOS EXECUTIVE

The MS-DOS EXECUTIVE is a program that will list all files and programs found in a given sub-directory and allow you to rename, delete or copy files, create new directories and get information on any file. It is supplied with Windows version 3.0 for compatibility with previous versions of Windows. Note that an even newer version is supplied with Windows version 3.1.

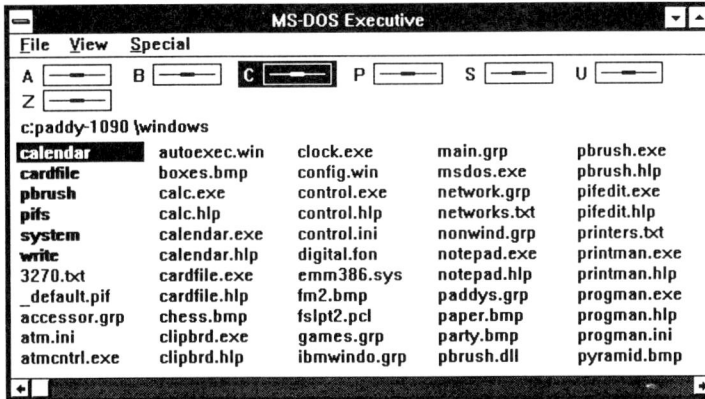

Figure 8.8 Windows version 3.0 MS-DOS Executive accessory.

It can be invoked in the same manner as SYSEDIT (it is called MSDOS.EXE) or you can create a program item for it in any program group (its icon appears as a 'floppy disk'). When creating a program item the following COMMAND LINE entry should be used:

```
C:\WINDOWS\MSDOS.EXE
```

PAINTBRUSH

You can only print colour images from PAINTBRUSH if you are using a colour PostScript printer or a Hewlett-Packard PaintJet printer. These are the only printers that currently recognise Device Independent Bit-maps (DIBs), the colour file format that PAINTBRUSH uses.

In addition, when running Windows version 3.0 in Real mode, you might receive out-of-memory messages when you try to print. If so, try one of the following:

(1) Close all other applications and try printing again.

(2) Save the PAINTBRUSH file and exit Windows. Start Windows again in Standard mode or 386 Enhanced mode, and then print the PAINTBRUSH file.

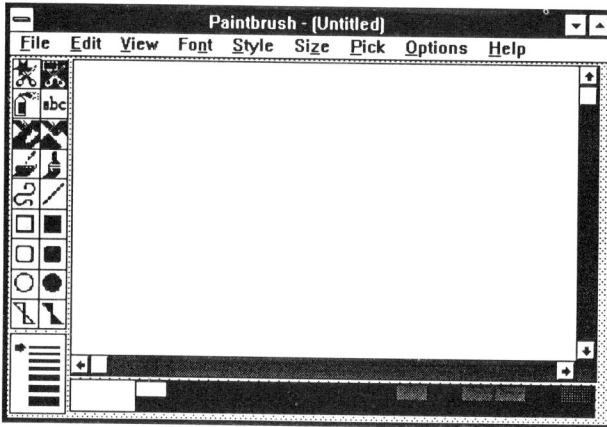

Figure 8.9 Window 3 PAINTBRUSH accessory.

If you can only run Windows in Real mode, you can convert the colour image and save it to a black and white format, then open the converted file and print the monochrome Bit-map.

PAINTBRUSH pictures can be saved in a file format called PCX which allows them to be transferred to DrawPerfect version 1.1.

If you have ever been frustrated by the fact that when you paste a screen dump (captured using Alt+PrintScreen or PrintScreen alone) into Paintbrush, the image, if too large, is clipped to the size of the Paintbrush area. To stop this simply select VIEW and then the ZOOM OUT option (or alternatively Ctrl+O) then PASTE in your image. If nothing appears then PASTE again. Zooming back in allows you to manipulate your image as normal.

PROGRAM MANAGER

The PROGRAM MANAGER is really the heart of the Windows environment, containing program groups which in turn contain the program items (or applications) that you run from your Windows environment.

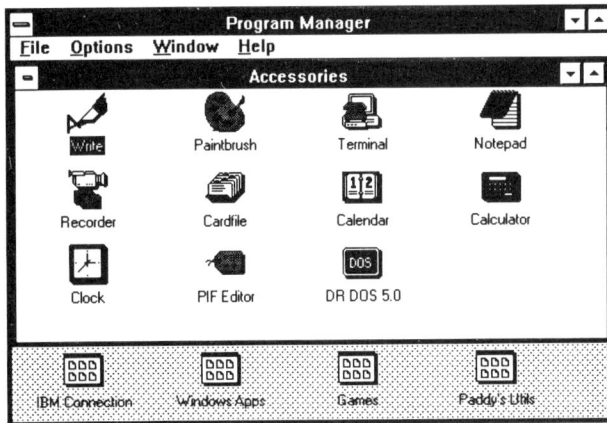

Figure 8.10 Windows PROGRAM MANAGER.

The PROGMAN.INI file contains information on and data about the selections made from within the Windows PROGRAM MANAGER. A typical PROGMAN.INI file contains two sections.

```
[Settings]
Window=34 0 542 389 1
AutoArrange=0

[Groups]
Group1=C:\WINDOWS\STARTUP.GRP
Order= 1 4 3 2 5
Group2=C:\WINDOWS\NONWINDO.GRP
Group3=C:\WINDOWS\BLUEBOOK.GRP
Group4=C:\WINDOWS\ACCESSOR.GRP
Group5=C:\WINDOWS\MAIN.GRP
```

Figure 8.11 Example Windows PROGMAN.INI file (version 3.1).

You can see in figure 8.11 that the user has created (with the PROGRAM MANAGER) an additional program group, called BLUEBOOK which is labelled group 3, alongside the standard Windows groups of Non-Window Applications, Accessories and Main.

Notice the STARTUP.GRP in figure 8.11. This is a new program group that has been added to simplify auto-starting applications under Windows version 3.1. By placing applications in this startup group (simply drag them from within Program Manager) they are executed every time Windows is started. This eliminates many, but not all, of the requirements for adding the applications to the LOAD and RUN statements in the WIN.INI file. When Windows is loaded, the applications that are installed in the startup group execute, one after another, in the order that they appear in the group.

It is not normally advisable to manually edit the PROGMAN.INI file but in some cases doing so can be of value. Take as an example the case where a network administrator would like a standard group (of applications, utilities and icons) to appear on his network users' Windows desktops. A very easy way to do this is to amend an individual user's PROGMAN.INI file and add a group that points to a group (simply a .GRP file that he has previously created and copied to a central shared network drive). In the example shown in figure 8.12, the S: drive is a shared network drive and group 5 has been manually added.

```
[Groups]

Group1=C:\WINDOWS\GAMES.GRP
Group2=C:\WINDOWS\NONWINDO.GRP
Group3=C:\WINDOWS\ACCESSOR.GRP
Group4=C:\WINDOWS\MAIN.GRP
Group5=S:\LAN\UTILS.GRP
```

Figure 8.12 PROGMAN.INI file amended by a network administrator.

MICROSOFT WORD FOR WINDOWS

In the sub-directory where you have installed Word for Windows, you will find a file called WINWORD.INI (the default is C:\WINWORD). This is not editable by any text editor, including the NOTEPAD accessory.

Word for Windows inserts a [Microsoft Word] section in the WIN.INI file. This typically consists of one or two sections, depending on whether you requested the ability to convert documents from other word processor formats.

```
[Microsoft Word]

CONVNUM=2
CONV1="Windows Write" C:\WINWORD\CONV-WRI.DLL ^.WRI
CONV2="WordPerfect 5.0" C:\WINWORD\CONV-WP5.DLL ^.DOC
Conversion=Yes
[WWFilters]
Windows Metafile=WMF.FLT,WMF
PCX Filter=PCXIMP.FLT,PCX
```

Figure 8.13 Example WIN.INI file section for Word for Windows.

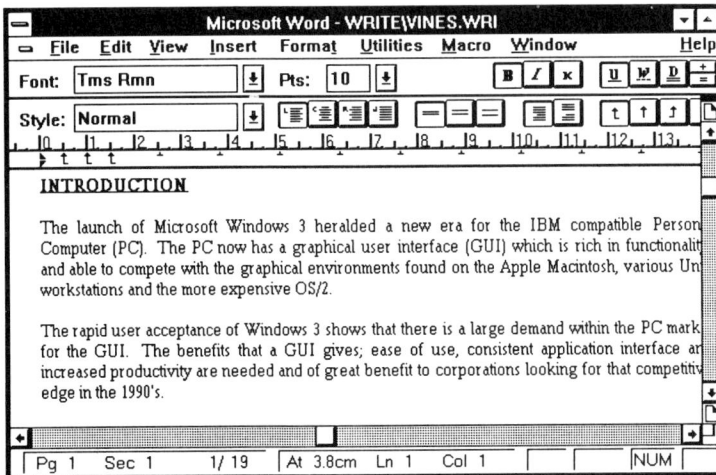

Figure 8.14 Microsoft Word for Windows.

- 115 -

Some printers require that you insert the following line in the [Microsoft Word] section of your WIN.INI file to ensure that they properly print underlining, word underlining, double underlining, or strikethrough:

```
UnderlineMode=1
```

With this line in your WIN.INI file, printing will be much slower, so insert this line only if your printer is not printing underlining properly.

MICROSOFT EXCEL

An EXCEL.INI file contains information on selections made from within Excel. There are several useful features and facilities that you can easily add and make use of.

You can force Excel to automatically move the cursor down one cell whenever a user presses enter by adding the following entry in the EXCEL.INI:

```
Entermove=1
```

You can also specify a file to be opened automatically whenever Excel is started up by adding the following entry:

```
OPEN=C:\EXCEL\WORK\MONEY.XLS
```

The file format of version 3.0 of Excel is now an Extended Biff format. The file extension has not changed. It is still .XLS, and Excel v3.0 is able to read and write old (Excel 2.x) Biff files but Excel 2.1 is unable to read or write Extended Biff. It is possible to keep files compatible with all earlier versions by entering in the SAVE AS dialog the Excel 2.1 format.

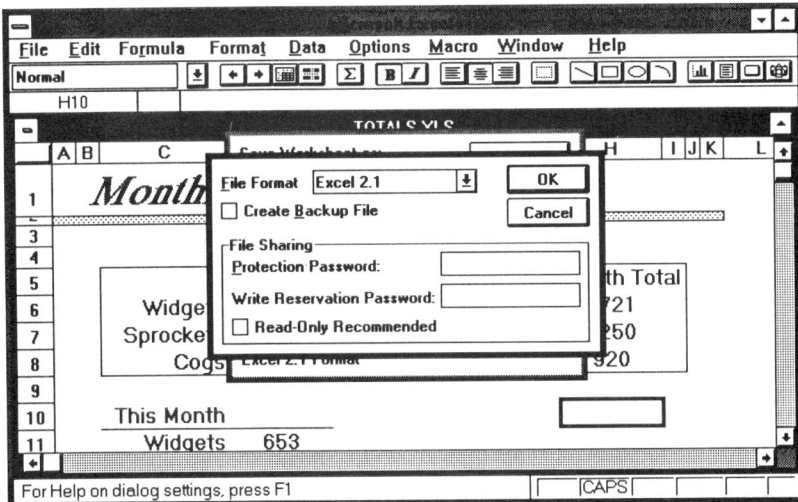

Figure 8.15 Saving Excel 3.0 files in Excel 2.1 Biff format.

Excel 3 has a new facility that allows users to launch it from a DOS directory other than the Excel application directory. This means that when a user chooses SAVE AS or FILE OPEN Excel will default to the launch directory. To use this useful feature change the Excel icon's properties to that shown in figure 8.16.

```
EXCEL.EXE - P C:\FINANCE
```

Figure 8.16 Changing the command line to allow a launch directory.

OBJECT LINKING AND EMBEDDING (OLE)

Object linking and embedding is an important component of Microsoft's strategy for the 1990s - that of "Information at your Fingertips". Amongst many other things, this basically means that PC systems evolve to the point where users are not even aware that different applications are being invoked to produce, say, a report. The user indicates what is to happen and the system does the rest.

Embedding is very similar to cutting and pasting data between applications, except that any embedded information is always still managed by the source application. If a user wished to update or change the embedded information they could do so from the application where the data had been embedded. Perhaps this is best described by use of an example.

A user wishes to insert a drawing into a piece of text. So whilst using an OLE word processor and after writing several pages of text, they decide to embed a drawing previously prepared from an OLE aware painting or drawing application. If they wished to alter the drawing they would not have to leave their word-processing application; they could simply click on the drawing and modify it in situ - using of course, all the features, commands and tools of the painting application.

It will soon be possible to embed and manipulate any type of information in any document regardless of source.

Linking is very similar to the current Dynamic Data Exchange (DDE) mechanisms of Windows at present. The process of Linking basically embeds information from one document into another without making a physical copy. For example, take a report with a list of figures. A user could copy the table of figures from its original file and manually track and adjust future changes. However, a better solution would be to link the report (being prepared by a word-processor) with the table (probably in a spreadsheet) so that table changes are reflected in the report automatically.

Links are maintained no matter where the original price list or the report is moved on the user system.

PACKAGER

Windows 3.1 includes a utility called PACKAGER that supports OLE. It allows users to take any file, link it to an icon and then embed that file (represented by the icon) into an application that supports OLE.

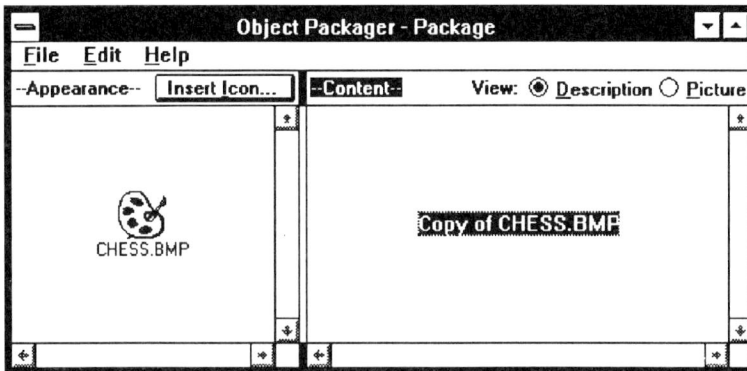

Figure 8.17 Windows version 3.1 object packager application.

The Windows system itself will be continuously improved and allow developers more scope in using OLE protocols in their applications, giving Windows users a much more intuitive and powerful interface.

CHAPTER

9

DISPLAY ADAPTERS

When designing Windows, Microsoft sensibly decided to make the product device independent. This means that Windows and correctly written application software is able to work with a wide variety of different hardware. This flexibility also extends itself into the video arena where Windows is able to run on screens ranging from CGA (Colour Graphics Adapter) through to Super-VGA.

For Windows to work with a display adapter a small but essential utility program called a Display Driver needs to be loaded. Display drivers for the more popular graphic adapters are supplied with Windows. However for the best results we recommend that you contact the manufacturer of your card to see if they have written their own. It is highly likely that the driver written by the manufacturer will be faster and be able to take advantage of the special features of your graphics adapter such as non-standard graphic modes and more colours.

DISPLAY ADAPTER TYPES

Since the initial launch of the IBM PC a number of graphics standards have been introduced, some more successful than others. The following is a description of display options available to users of Windows.

The technical descriptions are based on the minimum specifications for the different graphics adapters. You may find that some manufacturers have extended the facilities that their cards are able to offer.

IBM Colour Graphics Adapter (CGA)

Modes supported	Text	40 x 25
		80 x 25
	Graphics	320 x 200 in 4 colours
		640 x 200 in 2 colours

Palette	16 colours

In response to pressure from the PC users IBM introduced the Colour Graphics Adapter (CGA). CGA provides a low quality (by today's standards) colour text and graphic display. Each character on the screen is formed in an 8 x 8 pixel matrix (see figure 9.1) and as a result the text display lacks definition.

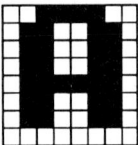

Figure 9.1 Example of the CGA text matrix.

CGA is mainly found on older PCs and some (also old) portable computers with liquid crystal displays (LCD). Although Windows will quite happily run on a CGA type display we do not recommend CGA for use with Windows.

Hercules Graphic Adapter (HGA)

Modes supported   Text   80 x 25

                             Graphics   720 x 348 in monochrome

Palette   N/A

The Hercules standard was introduced to provide graphics to users of monochrome monitors. Even though it lacks colour the high resolution graphics mode makes it a perfectly acceptable adapter for use with Windows. Unlike CGA, the characters in text mode are formed in an 8 x 14 pixel matrix (see figure 9.2). This allows the text to be displayed with far more definition.

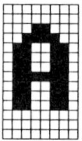

Figure 9.2 Example of the Hercules text matrix.

Hercules adapter cards are still popular with those people who do not require colour graphics: word-processor users and people involved in CAD/CAM. Most modern Video Graphics Array (VGA) cards are able to emulate the Hercules standard.

Enhanced Graphics Adapter (EGA)

Modes supported   Text   40 x 25

                                     80 x 25

                                     80 x 43

                           Graphics   320 x 200 in 16 colours

                                          640 x 200 in 16 colours

                                          640 x 350 in 2 colours

                                          640 x 350 in 16 colours

Palette   64 colours

In response to the request for higher resolutions and more colours the EGA standard was developed. EGA was the predecessor to the modern VGA cards and offers some very usable graphics and text modes. A special monitor, called a digital monitor, is required to display EGA colour graphics.

There are two serious limitations to the EGA standard: small colour palette and slow screen refresh speed. These, coupled with the introduction of the VGA standard from IBM, have meant that EGA has had a premature death.

EGA equipped machines are perfectly able to run Windows and the displays they produce are both crisp and colourful.

Video Graphics Array (VGA)

Modes supported	Text	As per EGA plus
		80 x 50
	Graphics	As per EGA plus
		320 x 200 in 256 colours
		640 x 480 in 2 colours
		640 x 480 in 16 colours

Palette   256,000

IBM decided that they wanted to introduce an enhanced display standard with their new PS/2 machines. Their answer, VGA, has become the most widely used graphics adapter in modern PCs. Whilst maintaining backward compatibility with CGA and EGA the

VGA standard goes on to increase the number of colours available on screen and also the vertical resolution.

The way the colours are produced has also changed. All previous display adapters were attached to digital monitors which limited the number of displayable colours on screen to sixteen. VGA uses analogue monitors which, in theory, allow for an almost infinite number of colours to be displayed. The increase of the palette to 256,000 colours reflects this new flexibility.

It is fair to say that VGA is *the* card to have for Windows. The colour graphics are quick (by PC standards!) and produce a bright and colourful display.

Super VGA

Modes supported	Text	As per VGA plus
		132 x 25
		132 x 43 etc
	Graphics	As per VGA plus
		640 x 480 in 256 colours
		800 x 600 in 16 colours
		800 x 600 in 256 colours
		1024 x 768 in 16 colours
		1024 x 768 in 256 colours etc
Palette		Up to 4,000,000+

Not content with VGA's highest resolution of 640 x 480 in 16 colours manufacturers looked for ways to enhance the VGA standard. These enhanced modes are known as Super VGA and can vary from adapter to adapter.

Nearly all Super VGA cards are able to support the standard VGA modes, and those with 1MB of video memory can support resolutions of up to 1024 x 768 pixels in 256 colours. You will need to obtain display drivers from the card's manufacturer for software to work in the enhanced modes. For this reason, when buying Super VGA cards we recommend that you purchase cards from established manufacturers such as IBM, Paradise, VEGA or Orchid.

IBM 8514/A

Modes supported	Text	80 x 25
	Graphics	640 x 480 in 256 colours
		1024 x 768 in 256 colours
Palette	262,144	

IBM's answer to the limitations of the VGA standard is (was?) the 8514/A video card. The 8514/A is a complete break with the previous graphic standards as no compatibility is included with previous standards such as VGA.
The lack of backward compatibility means that machines containing 8514/A cards must also have VGA adapters if they are to run all PC software. As you can imagine this can be expensive and can introduce numerous problems such as BIOS incompatibility.

Two other reasons why the 8514/A has not been a success is its lack of support for flicker-free non-interlaced displays and its MCA based architecture. However, the performance increase obtained from the onboard graphics co-processor is impressive and certainly of great benefit to users of Windows.

IBM Extended Graphics Array (XGA)

Modes supported	Text	As per VGA plus
		132 x 43
		132 x 50
		132 x 60
	Graphics	As per VGA plus
		640 x 480 in 65536 colours
		1024 x 768 in 2 colours
		1024 x 768 in 4 colours
		1024 x 768 in 16 colours
		1024 x 768 in 256 colours

Palette   Up to 4,000,000+

Once again, IBM have responded to the problems with their 8514/A adapter by introducing the Extended Graphics Array (XGA). Unlike the 8514/A, the XGA supports all the standard VGA modes.

The XGA card is an intelligent device containing its own graphics co-processor and 1MB of video RAM. IBM claim that XGA is 50-100% faster than a standard VGA card, achieved by combining 32 bit data access to the video RAM with internal display caching and the graphics co-processor.

Unfortunately IBM have still not provided support for non-interlaced displays although third party manufacturers have. The XGA is an excellent standard and deserves to do well in the PC video market.

INTERLACED VS. NON-INTERLACED DISPLAY

There are currently two methods, interlaced and non-interlaced, used to allow monitors to display resolutions of 1024 x 768 and beyond.

Interlaced

Interlaced is the method chosen by IBM for its 8514/A and XGA cards. The image is built from two passes of the electron beam over the phosphorous screen. The advantage of this method is cost, as the monitor technology required is relatively simple and therefore cheap.

Unfortunately an interlaced display suffers from flicker and a lack of clarity on all but the very best monitors. The acceptability of the flicker will rest with each individual user but at least the XGA card can support the more expensive non-interlaced monitors.

Non-interlaced

The best results with high resolution displays are obtained with non-interlaced cards and monitors. A non-interlaced image is built in one pass of the electron beam and is flicker-free.

As you can probably guess, the cost of such a display is high and the expense may only be justified for graphical power users such as those using CAD/CAM or Desktop Publishing software.

SCREEN REFRESH

A standard VGA display (640 x 480) is redrawn or refreshed 60 times every second. The refresh rate is measured in Megahertz. In simple terms the faster the screen refresh the less flicker that will be visible on the screen.

When choosing a video card for your PC you will notice that refresh rates vary with resolution. Figure 9.3 shows the typical refresh rates for each of the higher resolutions. Normally the higher the refresh rate the more expensive the card.

RESOLUTION	REFRESH RATES
800 x 600	56Hz, 60Hz, 70Hz, 72Hz
1024 x 768	43Hz, 60Hz, 70Hz, 72Hz, 76Hz

Figure 9.3 Typical refresh rates for the higher resolutions

You will find that refresh rates of 56Hz or less cause noticeable flicker on the monitor (particularly if a bright or white background is used). In an environment with fluorescent lights you will find that there is even more flicker when using a refresh rate of 60Hz or less.

Refresh rates of 70Hz and above, including the Video Electronics Standards Association (VESA) standard of 72Hz, are generally flicker-free. In some cases however, even if you use a board with this level of refresh rate and combine it with an interlaced monitor you may still notice flicker.

THE BEST COMBINATION

As we have seen, the best Windows display is a combination of two things: a flicker-free video card (or board) and a high resolution monitor. This will cause you the least amount of eye strain and provide you with the best possible desktop in order to run Windows and your applications.

One good thing about Windows is that as long as the video board manufacturer supplies a Windows device driver there are very few software compatibility problems to contend with. This means that you are free to choose any number of possible combinations for the price/performance you require. We would suggest that you try and get hold of a monitor that displays at least an 800 x 600 resolution image and a video card with the highest refresh rate that you can afford.

COLOUR VERSUS RESOLUTION

The answer to the colour versus resolution question can only be answered once you have decided what your PC is going to be used for. If you are going to be heavily involved in graphical work using programs like Corel Draw and Microsoft's Powerpoint then colours are likely to be more important.

On the other hand if you use AutoCAD or a similar package then you are likely to prefer resolution to colour. Our advice is to go for the 512K graphics card which can support a resolution of 800 x 600 in 256 colours. This configuration is suitable for 90% of uses and is unlikely to break the bank!

USING VGA DISPLAY ADAPTERS

If you use a VGA-compatible display adapter and have difficulties running Windows in 386 Enhanced mode, you might need to include the following line in the [386Enh] section of your SYSTEM.INI file:

```
EMMEXCLUDE=C400-C7FF
```

This is because some VGA compatible cards use additional memory to enhance the performance of their cards. Manufacturers of these cards include Video 7 and Paradise. Display adapter boards with the main chip(s) manufactured by Tseng Labs, Chips and Technologies, Paradise, and Headland Technologies also function this way.

When Windows is running in 386 Enhanced mode and is configured for VGA, Windows detects most of these cards and automatically excludes the additional memory. However, you must add the line to SYSTEM.INI yourself if:

o   You configured Windows for an 8514/A and have both an 8514/A and a VGA.

o   You have an enhanced VGA adapter that Windows does not recognise.

If you have both a VGA display adapter (primary) and an 8514/A (secondary), you might have problems switching between full-screen non-Windows applications when running Windows in 386 Enhanced mode.

If an application does not display properly, the digital to analog converter (DAC) on your VGA card needs to be updated. Contact the manufacturer for an upgrade.

In the meantime, if your application has a command to refresh the screen, you might be able to temporarily correct the display so you can use the application. For example, if your display is a colour display, you can type the following at the DOS Prompt and press ENTER:

```
MODE CO80
```

Further information about commands that refresh the screen can be found in your applications documentation.

USING SELF-CONFIGURING DISPLAY ADAPTERS

Some display adapters can change their configurations to match what an application tries to do. For example, if an application tries to use a VGA display, the adapter could switch from an EGA configuration to VGA. This type of display adapter makes use of non-maskable interrupts (NMIs) to re-configure itself as you work.

To use this type of display adapter with Windows running in 386 Enhanced mode, you must disable the NMI (self-configuring) option.

First configure the display adapter for the type of monitor you have, then disable the NMI option.

PARADISE VGA DEVICE DRIVERS

Paradise have made available various Windows drivers for their VGA cards. If you have a Paradise VGA card in your machine, you can obtain higher resolution by using one of their supplied drivers rather than the default VGA driver as supplied by Microsoft.

The Paradise VGA drivers currently available are:

    PVGA480.DRV - Paradise VGA 640 x 480 256-colour
    VGA800.DRV   - Paradise VGA 800 x 600 16-colour
    VGA1024.DRV - Paradise VGA 1024 x 768 16-colour

These can now be found supplied as standard with Windows version 3.1 (along with a new Microsoft default driver for 800x600 resolution for Super VGA which you may wish to try out). For users of Windows version 3.0 they should still be freely available either from your local computer dealer, direct from the manufacturer or can be found as part of the Microsoft Supplemental Drivers Library (SDL) diskettes.

The following instructions should be of interest to any reader as background information on how the drivers work but will only need to be followed for those users using Windows version 3.0:

You do not have to re-install Windows to change the display adaptors. If you do have Windows installed, leave the Windows environment and from a DOS prompt, change to the sub-directory where Windows is installed and type in SETUP. Then follow the instructions below.

If you have not yet installed Windows, run SETUP as normal and follow the instructions below when asked to confirm the hardware configuration.

(1) Select the DISPLAY option from the SYSTEM INFORMATION list using the up and down cursor keys and press ENTER.

(2) Scroll to the bottom of the list using the DOWN cursor key.

(3) Select OTHER and press ENTER.

(4) Type in the full pathname of the disk containing the new Paradise VGA drivers.

(5) Select the desired driver from the given list, according to your needs and hardware resolution.

(6) Choose ACCEPT CONFIGURATION SHOWN ABOVE and press the ENTER key.

If you are installing Windows for the first time, you will need to follow the screen messages to continue the Windows installation process. Some distribution disks containing the Paradise device drivers also contain a program called COLORS.EXE. This is a Windows program that will display all the colours available to your system with the driver you have chosen.

VIDEO SEVEN VEGA DEVICE DRIVERS

Video Seven have also made available three Windows drivers for their VEGA VGA cards. If you have a Video Seven VEGA VGA card in your machine you can obtain higher resolution by using one of their supplied drivers rather than the default VGA driver as supplied by Microsoft (although again you may wish to try the new Microsoft 800x600 default driver now suppled with Windows version 3.1).

The VEGA VGA drivers available are:

> V748016.DRV for 640 x 480 16 colour
> V754016.DRV for 720 x 540 16 colour
> V760016.DRV for 800 x 600 16 colour

These can now be found supplied as standard with Windows version 3.1. For users of Windows version 3.0 they should still be freely available either from your local computer dealer, direct from the manufacturer or can be found as part of the Microsoft Supplemental Drivers Library (SDL) diskettes.

The following instructions should be of interest to any reader as background information on how the drivers work but will only need to be followed for those users using Windows version 3.0.

If you already have Windows installed (using the default VGA display driver supplied with Windows), you can install a VEGA driver as follows:

(1) Choose the correct driver for the resolution you have available.

(2) Copy the V7xxxx.DRV file from the floppy disk into the SYSTEM sub-directory.

(3) Using the Windows NOTEPAD or SYSEDIT accessories edit the SYSTEM.INI file and change the DISPLAY.DRV= entry in the [Boot] section from:

```
DISPLAY.DRV=VGA.DRV TO DISPLAY.DRV=V7xxxx.DRV
```

Make any modifications as necessary. If you had installed Windows with the standard VGA driver you would need to make the above changes.

(4) Save the SYSTEM.INI file. Restart Windows from the MS-DOS command line. You should now be running in the resolution you chose.

If you do not have Windows installed, install Windows as normal but change the VGA display option to OTHER when asked to confirm the hardware configuration. Then, when prompted, insert the VEGA driver disk in drive A, press ENTER and then complete the installation as normal.

ACCELERATED DISPLAY CONTROLLERS

The popularity of Windows (and to a lesser extent the emergence of other graphical user interfaces) has prompted a great deal of interest in what are sometimes called GUI Accelerators but are more accurately known as Accelerated Display Controllers.

Most Windows users would agree that even the most powerful PCs on the market today would benefit from faster display performance. This should indicate that if the price is right, any product that gives faster display performance is going to be useful and will probably be bought by a lot of people.

Chip technology that accelerates graphical displays has been around for some time. It is currently most commonly found in high-end PCs or workstations that are designed for use with Computer Aided Design software or other graphical intensive applications.

The rapid emergence of Windows now provides the first high-volume opportunity for accelerated displays. The reason for this is two-fold.

First, DOS based applications typically write directly to the display hardware. This means that a non-standard display controller requires a custom device driver for each application it is to be used with. This is completely different to the Windows environment where applications do not access the display controller directly but instead call Windows services that in turn access an installed display device driver. Thus a single display device driver supports all Windows applications. Secondly, the sluggish performance of Windows screen handling, even when using some of the most powerful i486 CPU based systems, provides a strong incentive for accelerated display controllers. The current accelerated display controllers on the market are aimed at OEMs for use in the manufacture of their systems. The relatively cheap cost of an accelerated display controller coupled with the amazing performance benefits it can give are likely to make them standard features in all but low-end PCs.

Two manufacturers currently making accelerated display controllers are Weitek, with their W5086 user interface controller, and a company called S3 with their 86C911 display controller.

Obviously with any hardware product like this, backwards compatibility is very important. Both of these controllers are fully VGA compatible and allow all applications, even DOS applications that access hardware directly, to run without modification. Using the supplied Windows device drivers (and a monitor that supports the correct resolution) users will be able to display resolutions of either 1024x768 or 1280x1024 (using 512K and 1MB VRAM respectively) but with between 2 to 4 times performance improvements over standard VGA.

In an ever more competitive marketplace, and as OEMs seek to differentiate their PCs from their competitors, expect to see PC systems designed, badged and marketed as Windows workstations. The better ones of these will include the aforementioned accelerated display controllers.

CHAPTER

10

MISCELLANEOUS HINTS AND TIPS

This chapter describes solutions to general problems that you might have when running Windows and various Windows applications and also covers miscellaneous hints and tips.

INCREASING YOUR DISPLAY'S UPDATE SPEED

If a non-Windows application running in 386 Enhanced mode seems to be updating the display very slowly, try creating or modifying the application's program information file (PIF).

Check the application's PIF file to make sure none of the MONITOR PORT's check boxes are selected in the ADVANCED SETTINGS dialog box. On some displays, cancelling the MONITOR PORTS options might mean that you cannot switch back to the application after switching away. In this case, you must exit the first application before starting another.

USING COM PORTS FOR COMMUNICATIONS

If you are running a non-Windows application that uses COM ports for communications, you might lose characters or receive protection violations. If so, include the following setting in your SYSTEM.INI file:

```
COMxProtocol=XOFF
```

Where X is the number for the COM port. If the application continues to lose characters after this setting is made, you should try increasing the corresponding COMxBuffer value.

The COMxBuffer value specifies the number of characters that will be buffered by the device on the corresponding communications port. Buffering may slow down communications on a port but might be necessary to prevent some communications applications from losing characters at high baud rates. The size of the buffer required will depend on the speed of the machine and the application's needs so the only way to set this is by trial and error. The default is 128.

MOUSE PROBLEMS

A number of the problems that you are likely to get with mice are caused by hardware interrupt conflicts within your machine. If you experience problems with your mouse we suggest that you first check your interrupt assignments with a utility program such as Norton Utilities.

We have found through our experiences with Windows that you are likely to find considerably less problems if you use a Microsoft mouse.

SELECTING A PORT FOR A SERIAL MOUSE

Do not try to run your serial mouse from the COM3 or COM4 port. Windows supports serial mice on COM1 and COM2 only.

PROBLEMS WITH SETUP AND LOGITECH MICE

You may find if you choose LOGITECH SERIAL from the Windows SETUP, that the installation program goes further for a while and then just returns to the MS-DOS prompt. This is because the Windows SETUP program has either found a Bus Board in your computer, or thinks a Bus Board or Bus Port is present. It will not install Windows for a serial mouse if this is so.

You can work around this problem by restarting the SETUP program and choosing either a MOUSE SYSTEM or VISION mouse when prompted. This will enable you to use a Logitech serial mouse as long as the Logitech mouse driver is not loaded with the command MOUSE SER PC.

Other Logitech Mouse Problems

Other intermittent problems may arise when using Logitech mice. We have found that often when returning to the Windows PROGRAM MANAGER from a MS-MS-DOS application (quite often a communications or terminal emulation program), the mouse will no longer respond (and vibrates uncontrollably across the screen). This never happens when using a Microsoft mouse.

For your existing Logitech mice, there is a fix disk available from Logitech containing a new copy of the LMOUSE.DRV file.

This can be installed as follows:

(1) Copy the new LMOUSE.DRV file to your SYSTEM sub-directory.

(2) Run Windows and run the SETUP program, modifying the mouse choice and selecting the LOGITECH SERIAL entry.

Add the following to the end of your SYSTEM.INI file:

```
[Logimouse]

Type=2        (1 to select a bus mouse)
Port=1        (2 for COM2)
Buttons=3
Orientation=1
```

Save the file, leave Windows and restart. This should solve your problems.

Logitech Bus Mouse

Note that if you have a Logitech bus mouse on your computer, SETUP will identify it as a Microsoft or PS/2 mouse. This is correct as the Logitech bus mouse is compatible with the Microsoft mouse driver.

HIDDEN WINDOWS ICONS

With Windows version 3.0, when you add non-Windows Applications you are given by default only a choice of eight icons. These are all contained in the file PROGMAN.EXE.

Control   Winfile   Swapfile   Sysedit   Setup   Progman   Progman

Winfile   Swapfile   Sysedit   Setup   Progman   Progman

Setup   Progman

Figure 10.1 Some of the 'Hidden Icons' buried in the Windows system.

If you know where to look there are various other icons available, some of which are shown in figure 10.1. The filename shown underneath tells you where each icon can be found.

To choose a new icon with Windows version 3.0, select the application icon you wish to change, select FILE, then PROPERTIES. Choose 'Select Change Icon' and replace the default PROGMAN.EXE entry, as shown in figure 10.2, with CONTROL, SETUP, SYSEDIT, SWAPFILE or WINFILE.EXE as appropriate. Clicking through 'VIEW NEXT' shows you the icons available in that file.

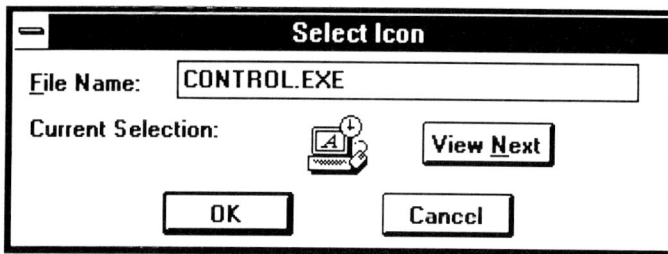

Figure 10.2 Windows 3.0 - 'Select Change Icon' and replace PROGMAN.EXE.

Changing the icons with Windows version 3.1 is much simpler. Figure 10.3 shows the method.

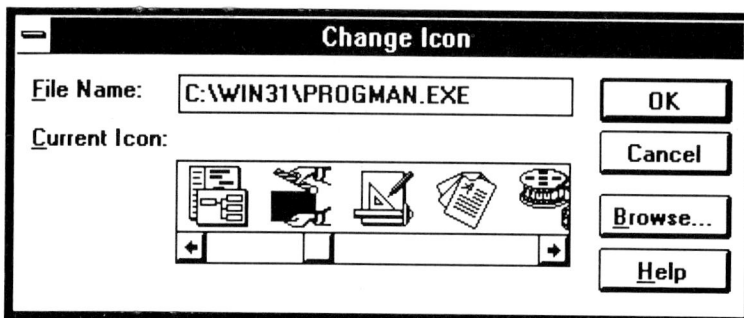

Figure 10.3 Windows 3.1 Change Icon dialog box.

The Change Icons push button takes you to (an improved) dialog box that shows you all the icons that are embedded in the appropriate Windows application. It also allows you to pick an icon (.ICO or .ICN) from a list of files. There are many more icons available within the Windows 3.1 environment, for example PROGMAN.EXE now contains over 40 different icons!

Remember, that you can also design your own icons with one of the many shareware icon editors available (Microsoft Visual Basic is supplied with an Icon Editor). Numerous icons can also be downloaded from a Windows conference bulletin board. Any of these can be used as an icon for both Windows and Non-Windows applications in the same manner as we outlined for replacing PROGMAN.EXE.

SMARTDRV.SYS

SMARTDRV.SYS is a disk-caching device driver (supplied by Microsoft) that operates with both MS-DOS and Windows. It minimises the number of times that your physical disks must be accessed by MS-DOS or Windows when it is running, since disks are relatively slow.

If you have installed SMARTDRV.SYS (and if you are using MS-DOS we strongly suggest that you do) you will be informed, when your machine boots up, that SMARTDRV.SYS has been installed and you will be given the version number of that particular SMARTDRV.SYS. The Windows 3.0 version of SMARTDRV.SYS is v3.03; however MS-DOS 5.0 is also supplied with a SMARTDRV.SYS v3.13. If you are using MS-DOS 5.0 (and of course Windows) make sure that your CONFIG.SYS file is correct and points to the new version of SMARTDRV; it is considerably faster than v3.03.

There are four ways that disk-caches normally cache disks: by sector, by cluster, by track or by cylinder.

SMARTDRV.SYS runs as a track cacher. When an application asks MS-DOS or Windows to read a sector of your disk, SMARTDRV intervenes and asks the disk-drive controller for the whole track that the sector resides on. SMARTDRV then passes the sector back to the application. This operation minimises head movement (which is fairly slow). Then, when the application asks for the next sector, SMARTDRV has it in its memory buffers and returns it immediately.

The major consideration when using SMARTDRV is that any high degree of file fragmentation destroys the benefits of any track cacher, since a particular file may be broken up inordinately across many tracks.

To minimise file fragmentation (and receive the full benefits of SMARTDRV) you must periodically unfragment your hard disk(s) using some form of disk-compaction program.

Some Windows applications, such as Qualitas 386MAX and Norton Desktop for Windows, supply disk-caching programs that can be used to replace SMARTDRV. Many users have successfully experimented with these third party disk cachers, replacing SMARTDRV with them. Often, depending on the particular machine and hard disk combination performance improvements can easily be made.

RAM DISK

Windows creates temporary work files as it runs. The files have a .TMP extension and are usually created in the TEMP sub-directory of your WINDOWS sub-directory. When you exit out of Windows these files are automatically deleted from your hard disk, thus reclaiming the space. However, it is possible for these files to be left behind if Windows crashes. We recommend that you check in the TEMP sub-directory periodically and delete any temporary files that are there.

One way to speed up Windows is to use a ram disk to store the temporary files that are created. As the files are created in ram they will automatically be deleted when the machine is turned off, thus simplifying housekeeping.

To install a ram disk and to inform Windows to change the location where it creates temporary files, changes are required to both the AUTOEXEC.BAT and CONFIG.SYS files.

Change the SET TEMP= line in the AUTOEXEC.BAT file (it probably points to C:\WINDOWS\TEMP or to a DOS\TEMP sub-directory) to SET TEMP=D:\ (D: being ram disk). Then insert the statement DEVICE=C:\DOS\RAMDRIVE.SYS xxx /E in the CONFIG.SYS file. Substitute the xxx with the required size of the ram disk.

CD-ROM EXTENSIONS

For various reasons MS-DOS and DR-DOS operating systems do not know how to access CD-ROM drives. CD-ROM drives, for example, use the High Sierra file format, do not include a File Allocation Table and have a drive sector size of 2048 bytes (most MS-DOS based disk drives use a sector size of 512 bytes). Due to these differences, CHKDSK, FORMAT and a few other MS-DOS utilities will not work on a CD-ROM DRIVE. The beauty of CD-ROM is that it can hold so much data on one disk, between 540-600MB. Many people already use CD-ROM in order to easily reference large amounts of data. Software vendors also may wish to supply complete applications and the appropriate technical manuals and publications on one easy-to-use CD.

The Microsoft CD-ROM Extensions (MSCDEX) allow an interface between the MS-DOS operating system, a CD-ROM device driver and a CD-ROM drive. These extensions are easily installed in a system by means of a terminate and stay resident program called MSCDEX.EXE.

In most cases, if you have installed the Microsoft CD-ROM Extensions correctly, Windows (including the File Manager) will work okay with your CD-ROM drive with no modifications or adjustments needed. Figure 10.3, shows our NEC CDR-75 CD-ROM player, known as drive D:, from File Manager. Note the different icon used to represent a CD-ROM drive as opposed to a floppy disk or hard drive.

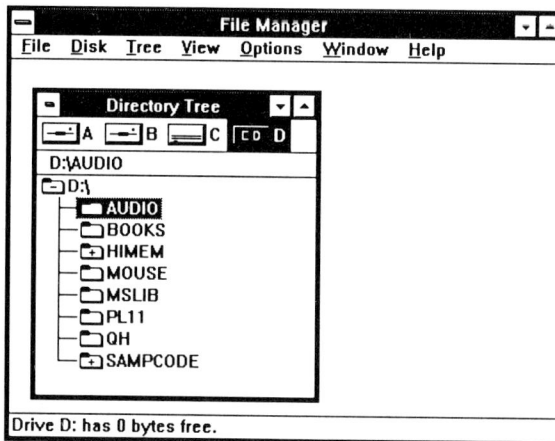

```
┌──────────────────────────────────────────────────────┐
│ ▬                       File Manager              ▼ ▲ │
│ File  Disk  Tree  View  Options  Window  Help         │
│                                                        │
│  ┌───────────────────────────────┐                    │
│  │ ▬        Directory Tree    ▼ ▲ │                    │
│  │ [▬·]A [▬·]B [══]C [CD·D]       │                    │
│  │ D:\AUDIO                       │                    │
│  │ ▭D:\                           │                    │
│  │       ├─■ AUDIO                │                    │
│  │       ├─▭ BOOKS                │                    │
│  │       ├─⊞ HIMEM                │                    │
│  │       ├─▭ MOUSE                │                    │
│  │       ├─▭ MSLIB                │                    │
│  │       ├─▭ PL11                 │                    │
│  │       ├─▭ QH                   │                    │
│  │       └─⊞ SAMPCODE             │                    │
│  └───────────────────────────────┘                    │
│ Drive D: has 0 bytes free.                             │
└──────────────────────────────────────────────────────┘
```

Figure 10.4 D: is an NEC CD-ROM Player and can be used in a normal manner.

If you have any problems using the CD ROM Extensions or your CD-ROM player with Windows then try the following:

o   Copy the file LANMAN10.386 from your Windows installation diskettes (it's normally found on disk #4) to the SYSTEM sub-directory where you installed Windows.

o   Add the following entry to the [386Enh] section of your SYSTEM.INI file:

```
DEVICE=LANMAN10.386
```

o   Finally, you will need to activate the drive by sending it a command before you start Windows. For example, in your AUTOEXEC.BAT file add the following before starting Windows:

```
DIR X:
```

Where x is the drive letter for the CD ROM drive.

This should take care of any problems.

SCSI HARD DISKS

If your system has a SCSI hard disk and you have any problems with Windows then try adding the following in the [386Enh] section of SYSTEM.INI:

```
VirtualHDIrq=OFF
```

The default setting is on and when set it allows Windows (in 386 Enhanced mode) to terminate interrupts from the hard disk controller rather than pass them onto a ROM routine that would normally handle these interrupts.

Many SCSI hard disks require that this setting be disabled so that all interrupts are handled (as they should be) by the ROM routine. Note that this slows down system performance so do not disable this setting unless you absolutely need to.

USING RLE FILES AS WALLPAPER

Files ending with a .RLE extension are traditionally in a graphics file format. RLE stands for Run-Length Encoded. You may sometimes see mention made of RLE-4, this is simply Run Length Encoded 4-bit.

RLE format graphics are much more efficient in terms of disk space (meaning of course that they also load quicker) than the more familiar bitmap (BMP) format. To give you some idea of a size comparison, we have several bitmap files that are about 273,662 bytes in length. Using a shareware utility, such as WinGIF, that allows you to convert a bitmap format file into RLE format, makes these files just 37,770 bytes long. This is a big saving in hard disk space!

An undocumented feature of Windows and the Windows Control Panel is that these RLE files can be used as wallpaper.

In the Desktop section of the Control Panel, place the mouse pointer on the text input box for wallpaper and click. All you need to do now is enter the full name (including the .RLE extension) of the file you wish to use as wallpaper and hit return.

Do not be put off by the fact that you are unable to list *.RLE files, however hard you try, using the Desktop part of the Control Panel. Using RLE files for wallpaper works exceptionally well, is very efficient and saves on a lot of disk space.

N.B. **At present the Windows Paintbrush cannot handle RLE format files.**

CREATING RLE FILES

To create your own RLE file, use Windows Paintbrush to create a graphics file no larger than 640 x 480 (640 x 250 for EGA systems) and save it as a BMP. Make sure that in the image you have no more than 16 colours.

Once you have converted it into RLE format (as mentioned earlier this can easily be done using one of the many shareware utilities available, such as WinGIF) you have a file suitable for use as a start-up screen or a (faster and smaller) Windows wallpaper.

Note that some RLE files may not be suitable for use as start-up screens because they are too large (over 55K) or too complex. If this is the case, either you will receive a 'Program too large to fit in memory' error message when you attempt to start up Windows or your graphics will not display correctly.

REPLACING THE MICROSOFT WINDOWS LOGO

It is possible to replace the Windows loading screen with one of your own; one such use may be to display a company logo. The files that are relevant to this process are stored in the WINDOWS sub-directory and are as follows:

WIN.COM	This starts Windows.
WIN.CNF	Loader part of WIN.COM.
VGALOGO.LGO	is the logo used by all VGA systems.
VGALOGO.RLE	is the compressed bitmap copy of the logo.

All that is required is to replace the VGALOGO.RLE file with one of your own and then bind this into the WIN.COM program. Before you attempt to do this we suggest you make backup copies of the above files.

You can create your own logo using PAINTBRUSH if you wish but you must save it as a 16 colour bitmap file (BMP). You must also compress this bitmap by using some form of utility to convert it into RLE-4 format. There are numerous shareware utilities around that do this, including WINGIF and PAINTSHOP.

The next stage is to attach your new loading screen to the WIN.COM program. From an MS-DOS prompt in the Windows SYSTEM sub-directory enter the following command:

```
COPY /B WIN.CNF+VGALOGO.LGO+NEWLOGO.RLE MYWIN.COM
```

The /B switch tells MS-DOS that the files should be copied in binary format and that the pluses concatenate the three files together to form MYWIN.COM. From now on whenever you type MYWIN to run Windows your loading screen will be displayed. It is perfectly acceptable to call your new file WIN.COM and in so doing replace the standard Windows loading program.

READABILITY OF ON-SCREEN FONTS

We found through trial and error that the fonts supplied with Windows for IBM's 8514 monitor were much clearer and easier to read than the default VGA fonts. It is worth your trying them yourself to see if you like them. If you do not it is easy enough to swop back to your old fonts.

First of all, if the 8514 fonts are not on your hard disk you will need to get them off the install diskettes. The easiest way to do this is to run SETUP from within Windows and change the video display to 8514/a. You will then be prompted to insert one of your Windows install diskettes. Once this is done choose the exit to MS-DOS option.

Now you are outside of Windows, change to your Windows directory and enter SETUP again. Change the video display (again) back to what you had before (most probably VGA), as this will allow you to get back into Windows.

You now need to edit your SYSTEM.INI file. You can do this either from Windows or from MS-DOS. Make a copy of your SYSTEM.INI file and change the following settings...

```
fixedfon.fon=vgafix.fon
oemfonts.fon=vgaoem.fon
fonts.fon=vgasys.fon
```

so that they point to the 8514 fonts...

```
fixedfon.fon=8514fix.fon
oemfonts.fon=8514oem.fon
fonts.fon=8514sys.fon
```

Once you have saved SYSTEM.INI and restarted Windows you should see the new 8514 fonts. If you do not like them then simply delete SYSTEM.INI, and replace with the backup you made earlier and you will be the same as before.

RUNNING WINDOWS WITH OS/2 VERSIONS 1.x

Windows version 3.0 runs quite comfortably with the OS/2 version 1.2 and 1.3 MS-DOS Compatibility Mode, albeit only in Real mode. This means that you cannot run non-Windows applications under the control of Windows in the MS-DOS compatibility box.

One thing to be careful with, in your OS/2 CONFIG.SYS mouse statement, is to make sure it says MODE=B, which allows the mouse to work in both Presentation Manager and the MS-DOS box. Quite often you will find the mode statement either not present or set to MODE=P (PM only).

Windows can be invoked from the MS-DOS box in three ways:

(1) Create an AUTOEXEC.BAT file that contains:

```
WIN /R
```

Whenever you go into the MS-DOS mode (DOS box), Windows will be started up automatically.

(2) From MS-DOS mode, manually enter WIN /R or create a batch file (BAT) to invoke Windows for you.

(3) Invoke Windows from an icon declared in an OS/2 PROGRAM MANAGER group.

Installing Windows under OS/2

Windows SETUP will only run under MS-DOS; you can temporarily boot up under MS-DOS or run it in the OS/2 MS-DOS box.

If you do run SETUP in an OS/2 MS-DOS box, do not allow Windows to make changes to your CONFIG.SYS file (and AUTOEXEC.BAT file). It is best to make the appropriate changes yourself.

If you have temporarily booted under MS-DOS (using a MS-DOS boot-up floppy disk or OS/2's Dual-Boot facility), it is quite safe to allow SETUP to make changes to your configuration files.

Printing from Windows under OS/2

The most important thing to remember is that if you wish to print, you must set the printer driver port to one with an .OS2 extension as follows:

If your printer is physically connected to LPT1 or to LPT2, then when you configure your printer, make sure you set the printer-driver port to LPT1.OS2 or LPT2.OS2.

If the printer is physically connected to LPT3 or LPT4, you must create a line for LPT3.OS2 or LPT4.OS2 in the [ports] section of your WIN.INI file and then set the printer driver to the appropriate .OS2 port when you configure it.

Using Windows Terminal under OS/2

Terminal will quite happily communicate through COM ports from an OS/2 1.x MS-DOS compatibility mode but you must set the port before you start Windows. To do this, you can run the SETCOM command from the MS-DOS prompt or you can include the initialisation in your OS/2 CONFIG.SYS file.

To set the COM port from the MS-DOS prompt, type the following before you start Windows:

```
SETCOM40 COMx=ON
```

For example, if you want to use COM1, you would type the following command:

```
SETCOM40 COM1=ON
```

To set the COM port automatically, you can add a line in your CONFIG.SYS file (more information on this can be found in your OS/2 documentation).

UNRECOVERABLE APPLICATION ERRORS (UAEs)

Unrecoverable Application Errors (UAE) should only occur in standard or 386 Enhanced modes. A UAE indicates that a Windows application has caused a protection violation. A protection violation is where a program has written to an area of memory to which it does not have access.

Obviously this could potentially corrupt other code or data in that area of memory. This is why after you receive a UAE your Windows system will be unstable. You should immediately close down all currently executing applications and exit Windows immediately.

There are many possible causes for UAEs. The following sections attempt to highlight some of them and give you clues to tracking down others.

CONFIG.SYS Files Statement

Many UAEs can be avoided by setting the FILES= setting in a user's CONFIG.SYS file to a high value. We suggest that if you experience any UAEs that you initially amend this CONFIG.SYS setting to FILES=60.

Windows 2.x Applications

Many applications that were designed for Windows versions 2.x can cause UAEs in a system if a user is running them in Windows Standard or 386 Enhanced mode. The reason for this is that the applications will not have been written for, and therefore will not be able to handle, the protected mode of both the Intel microprocessors and the Windows operating environment.

If an application was designed for Windows version 2.x then you will be alerted via a dialog box whenever you execute it. Version 2.x applications should only be run in Windows Real mode, as the dialog box will suggest.

Incorrect MS-DOS Version

If you are not using DR-DOS then you must make sure that machines running Windows are running the correct version of MS-DOS for that hardware type. By that we mean the OEM version of MS-DOS, such as Compaq MS-DOS, should only be used on the respective OEM hardware platforms.

As a general rule, if your hardware manufacturer has an OEM version of MS-DOS it should be used. If the manufacturer does not have an OEM version of MS-DOS then you should use either generic MS-DOS or DR-DOS.

Page-mapping Conflicts

If you are experiencing UAEs and are running in 386 Enhanced mode it is possible that you have a page mapping conflict (these only appear in 386 Enhanced mode). If possible, run your machine in standard mode for a while (WIN /S) and if UAEs do not occur then it is most likely that you do in fact have a page mapping conflict.

Page mapping conflicts occur in the adaptor segment area of memory (between hexadecimal A000 and EFFF). To further determine whether you have a page mapping conflict insert the following line in the [386enh] section of the SYSTEM.INI file.

```
EMMExclude=A000-EFFF
```

If, after restarting Windows, inserting this line solves your UAEs then you need to determine the position of all hardware adaptors in the adaptor segment and exclude them specifically (rather than excluding the entire region). You should not leave the whole range of memory (A000-EFFF) excluded as this is only used to test for the possibility of device conflicts. Leaving this set will greatly hamper system performance.

If you are using a Micro Channel Architecture (MCA) based machine then it is quite easy to determine all adaptor locations by booting up the machine with the machine's reference diskette.

If you are using the more standard ISA bus machine then you will need to consult all your adaptor card documentation for the memory locations used.

Unfortunately even when you know all the adaptor locations, finding the adaptor segment to specifically exclude is a case of trial and error.

Incompatible TSRs

It is quite common for terminate and stay resident (TSR) routines to be the cause of sporadic UAEs. If you suspect TSRs are causing you problems then you should temporarily remove all device drivers and TSR programs from your CONFIG.SYS and AUTOEXEC.BAT files to bring your system to a minimum configuration for testing purposes.

Obviously, if by doing this you eliminate UAEs then the problem was caused by one of the device drivers or TSRs you removed. You should carefully replace the removed lines one by one until the problem reappears. This will indicate to you which line is causing the problem.

RAM Shadowing

Many machines support RAM shadowing. Very occasionally this can be the root cause of UAEs. If nothing else works in removing UAEs then you should disable RAM shadowing to see if this helps.

Hardware Setup

We have already seen in Chapter 1 on installation that the Windows hardware detection mechanism can be disabled during SETUP by using a /I switch which can be useful if users are having difficulty in getting Windows installed on their hardware.

There are however many machines from various manufacturers that must be specifically selected in Windows SETUP in order for them to function correctly. Not selecting them is the biggest cause of hardware problems with Windows.

This list of machines can be found by running SETUP from outside Windows (you will not see them by invoking the SETUP icon from within Windows) and when presented with the system information selecting COMPUTER. Alternatively you can browse the file SETUP.INF and look for the [machine] section. The hardware currently found in this section is shown in figure 10.4.

All 80386 and 80486 based AST machines
All 80386 based Zenith machines
All Hewlett-Packard machines
Everex Step 386/25
NCR PC386SX
NCR PC 925
NEC PowerMate SX Plus
NEC ProSpeed 386
Toshiba 1600
Toshiba 5200

Figure 10.4 Machines that must be specifically selected in Windows SETUP.

If you look closely at the settings in the SETUP.INF [machine] section you will see entries that ensure that the Windows installation process adds settings such as EMMEXCLUDE and VirtualHDIrq to the SYSTEM.INI file. This is one of the reasons why these machines must be specifically selected in order for them to work correctly with Windows.

THE UAE AND MICROSOFT SUPPORT

Microsoft have made available two programs that are designed to aid Microsoft programmers in debugging the Windows system, i.e. finding out the root causes of UAEs or system hangs when reported by a user.

These two programs are, DrWatson which logs information about conditions that exist when an unrecoverable application error (UAE) occurs during a user's Windows session, and MSD (Microsoft Diagnostics) that identifies system configuration information.

A user who has been having problems with UAEs or other mysterious errors or crashes, should install both of these applications on his system and make sure that DrWatson is loaded whenever Windows is running (place it as a LOAD= statement in WIN.INI or simply drag it to the Windows 3.1 STARTUP.GRP). Whenever a UAE occurs DrWatson will write out error information to a log.

In order to help Microsoft identify and solve system problems (and in particular UAEs) Microsoft ask that you periodically send them any DrWatson logs that result.

Both DrWatson and MSD are available free of charge . Either your local dealer may have copies or they can be downloaded from Compuserve (DRWTSN.ZIP) or other bulletin boards. They are now supplied with Windows version 3.1.

Dr Watson

As we have already briefly mentioned, DrWatson is a debugging tool designed to provide software programmers with detailed information on the internal state of Windows when a UAE occurs. DrWatson must be running at the time a UAE occurs to extract the internal information from the system.

As DrWatson uses very little memory and does not affect the performance of Windows, Microsoft encourage users to install DrWatson if a UAE has occurred before. After DrWatson is installed, information is collected when a UAE occurs and written to a special file (DRWATSON.LOG) located in the Windows directory.

Remember that DrWatson is a diagnostic tool and not a cure for a problem. Having DrWatson will not prevent an error from occurring, but the information in DRWATSON.LOG will help Microsoft developers make the next version of Windows even better.

Microsoft Diagnostics (MSD)

The Microsoft Diagnostics (MSD) program is designed to assist Microsoft customers and Product Support Services (PSS) technicians in solving problems with Microsoft products. MSD identifies system configuration information such as the BIOS, video card type and manufacturer, installed processor(s), I/O port status, operating system version, environment settings, hardware devices attached, and additional software running concurrently with MSD.

MSD is designed to run in conjunction with DrWatson to provide valuable information on hardware configurations and UAEs. Error reports to send to Microsoft should include information from both the MSD program and DrWatson.

The documentation supplied with DRWTSN.ZIP includes much more information on DrWatson and MSD and how they can be used. We suggest that if you are having problems with UAEs, get hold of these applications, use them and send any error logs to Microsoft .

BIOS DATA

If you have to report problems, either to Microsoft or to your hardware manufacturer, you may need to know details about the BIOS in your machine. If details cannot be found in the documentation that came with your machine and you do not have access to MSD, then the following may help.

The name of the BIOS will always appear when you first boot up your machine, normally together with a version number. This version number will normally be enough for technical support people to distinguish it apart from other BIOSs in that computer range. Sometimes, however, you may need the date of the BIOS. This can quite easily be found by using MS-DOS DEBUG command as follows...

o   Enter DEBUG from a MS-DOS command Prompt.

    You will then be presented with an underscore. DEBUG is now waiting for you to enter a command.

o   Type D F000:FFF0 and press enter (spaces and upper case are important).

You will then be presented with a long row of figures. The figure on the far right hand side of the screen is the BIOS date.

LAPTOP AUTO RESUME

The better laptop and notebook Personal Computers have some form of AutoResume feature. This is the ability to turn the PC's power off without exiting from a software application and then return to that same software application when the power is turned back on.

This works fine with plain DOS but when Windows is involved the AutoResume feature can be erratic and in many PC implementations simply does not work.

A few laptop and notebook manufacturers supply some form of device driver to allow their AutoResume feature to work with Windows. For example, Toshiba supply a device driver that allows the AutoResume feature on their T2000SX and T3100SX computer to work with Windows. If you use a laptop or notebook, check with your manufacturer to see if they provide similar Windows AutoResume functionality.

The Toshiba device driver (generically called WINRES) can be obtained from your local Toshiba dealer, from Toshiba direct or downloaded from Compuserve (WINRES.ZIP). It consists of two files:

> BIOSXLAT.386 - A virtual mode device driver for Windows 3.
> WINRESUM.DOC - Associated documentation.

Unfortunately this device driver does not support Toshiba's AutoResume feature when running in Windows Real or Standard mode - it only works in 386 Enhanced mode.

Installation is simple and involves copying the file BIOSXLAT.386 to the Windows sub-directory and then editing SYSTEM.INI to replace the single occurrence of:

```
device=*biosxlat
```

with

```
device=biosxlat.386
```

This AutoResume driver is automatically loaded each time you launch Windows and will allow the AutoResume feature to function correctly whenever a normal power-off occurs.

ADVANCED POWER MANAGEMENT

Future versions of Windows will incorporate support for power management features that will soon be common in everyday PCs (typically notebook and laptop models - often using the Intel386SL microprocessors).

In battery powered PCs, battery life can be prolonged significantly by turning off devices or system components which are not needed at a particular time. This decision to turn devices on or off is usually made by the system BIOS. However, the operating system can help the BIOS make better power management decisions by communicating certain state information (such as the fact that an application is idle) to the BIOS. Similarly, the operating system can take specific actions if notified by the BIOS of some power management event (such as low battery power).

All this sounds rather complicated, and until recently was either not implemented at all or was carried out haphazardly in today's notebook and laptop computers. Intel and Microsoft got together and proposed a specification for a BIOS interface which establishes a co-operative environment between an operating system and its BIOS partner. This specification is called Advanced Power Management (APM).

APM will be implemented by various PC manufacturers in the form of a device driver which the operating system will install if it detects the existence of a compatible BIOS.

In the case of Windows, this power management device driver would be installed by adding a POWER.DRV statement to the SYSTEM.INI file. On successful installation of this device driver, its presence will be acknowledged to the user through a "Power Management" icon in the Windows Control Panel.

For those users running Windows on notebook and laptop computers, extending battery life is of the utmost importance. APM should greatly improve the functionality and usefulness of the portable computer and bring truly mobile computing ever closer.

CHAPTER

11

END-USER DEVELOPMENT

Today's PC users are more than just people who utilise spreadsheets, wordprocessors and databases. More often than not they are looking for ways to tailor their environment and the packages that run in it by use of macro and simple programming languages.

Microsoft are leading the way by adding to all their Windows applications a comprehensive and easy to learn macro language. They have also released Visual Basic, a powerful and easy-to-use Windows development tool.

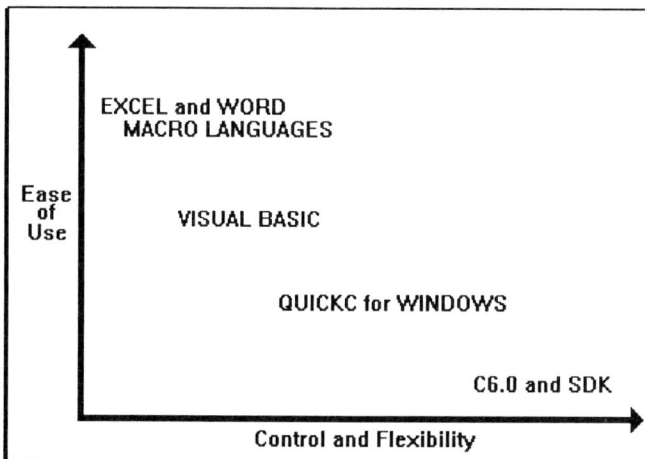

Figure 11.1 Microsoft's Windows tool strategy.

Figure 11.1 outlines Microsoft's Windows development tool strategy. At one end you have the macro languages that come with Excel and Word, and for those users who need a bit more flexibility or for corporate developers you have Visual Basic.

Also for corporate developers but mainly targeted at professional developers you have available both QUICKC for Windows and the combination of the Windows Software Developer's Kit and the Microsoft C 6.0 (and now C 7.0) compilers.

This chapter discusses two of the tools available to end-users that allow them to develop their own applications.

First, we will look at the de facto standard Windows spreadsheet - Microsoft Excel. Although Excel is not designed for the creation of major software systems on a PC, it is still possible to produce simple yet powerful Dialogs and application systems with it.

Secondly we will take a quick look at Visual Basic, and in particular how it can work together with Excel using DDE.

EXCEL DIALOGS

Microsoft Excel was one of the first graphical based spreadsheets on the market. It first appeared on the Apple Macintosh back in 1985 and fast became the most popular and best selling package for this (then unique) graphical environment.

Microsoft Excel for Windows is easily the most powerful spreadsheet and is again becoming a de facto standard for spreadsheets in a graphical environment.

All applications, such as Microsoft Word, Excel, Powerpoint etc., that are built for a graphical user interface such as Windows, make extensive use of the mouse and provide the user with buttons, action bars, Dialog boxes and List boxes that make the user interface friendlier, intuitive and easier to use.

Excel, as a spreadsheet, is pretty unique in that it allows users to create many of these resources using the standard Excel macro language and the supplied Dialog Editor. In the Windows world, programmers refer to icons, dialogs, radio buttons, check boxes, list boxes and the most familiar OK and Cancel type buttons as resources.

Push Buttons

The easiest resource to add to a spreadsheet is a simple push button. Push buttons can be any shape and any size, a simple one (called 'Picture It') is shown embedded in the spreadsheet shown in figure 11.2.

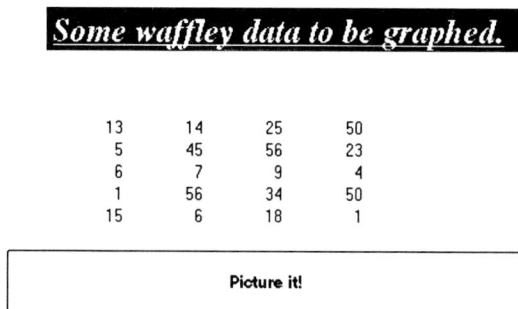

Some waffley data to be graphed.

13	14	25	50
5	45	56	23
6	7	9	4
1	56	34	50
15	6	18	1

Picture it!

Figure 11.2 Simple Push Button Placed in a Spreadsheet.

It is possible to program push buttons to do almost anything: to bring up other spreadsheets, to invoke macros which might, for example, draw a graph, or perhaps initiate Dynamic Data Exchange (DDE) links to other applications.

When the cursor is moved over a button on a spreadsheet, the cursor automatically changes to a 'pointing hand', thus showing users of that spreadsheet where the buttons are.

In order to create a push button on a spreadsheet using version 3.0 of Excel, do the following:

(1) Select the button tool on the toolbar.

(2) Point and drag the mouse pointer on the spreadsheet to create a button of required size. (Square buttons can be created by simultaneously holding down the SHIFT key.)

(3) At this stage, an Assign Macro dialog box will appear asking for the name of the command macro which will be assigned to this button. Select the required command macro or type a macro name or cell reference in the Reference Box. (Select Cancel if you wish to leave the macro assignment to later.)

(4) Add the text desired for the button by simply selecting the text currently on the button, and then editing it as usual. This text can have any font, size colour etc. as normal.

The button can be resized or moved in the usual way using mouse point and drag.

To assign the name of a macro to an existing button, simply select the button and then choose Macro Assign To Object from the Macro menu option. Use the Assign Macro dialog box as previously described above.

Dialog Editor

The Dialog Editor is supplied with every copy of Excel. If you do not have it already installed as an icon in your system then it can be found as program C:\EXCEL\EXCELDE.EXE. Once invoked, the Dialog Editor looks like that shown in figure 11.3.

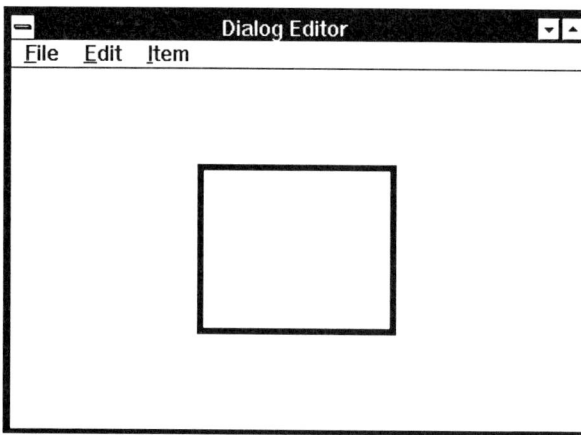

Figure 11.3 The Microsoft Excel Dialog Editor.

Dialog boxes are generally used by applications to ask or prompt users for additional information. This is then used (by the application) so that it can carry out some action or command.

The Dialog Editor is different from more normal Windows' editors since there are no Save options on any of the action bar menus. This often confuses first time users. As soon as a dialog box has been built it must be incorporated into a macro sheet before closing the dialog editor, or before creating a new dialog box, since either of these two actions will destroy any current dialog box definition.

Building a Dialog Box

The facilities available for building dialog boxes include, amongst others, adding buttons, text fields and informative icons and resizing and reshaping the box.

Information about the dialog box items (that are being added) can be obtained by selecting the required item in the dialog box and then selecting Info from the Edit menu option. One can also simply double-click on the item to obtain the same information. The information presented, which can be manually changed, includes items such as x-y coordinates, associated text, initial value and so on. The x-y values are often useful when attempting to line up different items, for instance an OK button with a Cancel button, which can be awkward when only using the mouse.

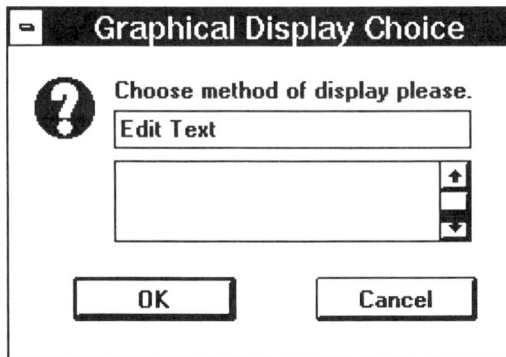

Figure 11.4 Simple Dialog Box built with the Excel Dialog Editor.

When a dialog has been built, the Select Dialog option on the Edit menu needs to be chosen (not the Select All option, which is a common mistake), followed by the Copy option.

This copies the relevant co-ordinates and details of the dialog to the Windows Clipboard. These details include such things as the size of the dialog box, associated text and initial or result values for each item.

This information should then be Pasted into the required cells in an open Excel macro sheet, an example of which is shown in figure 11.5.

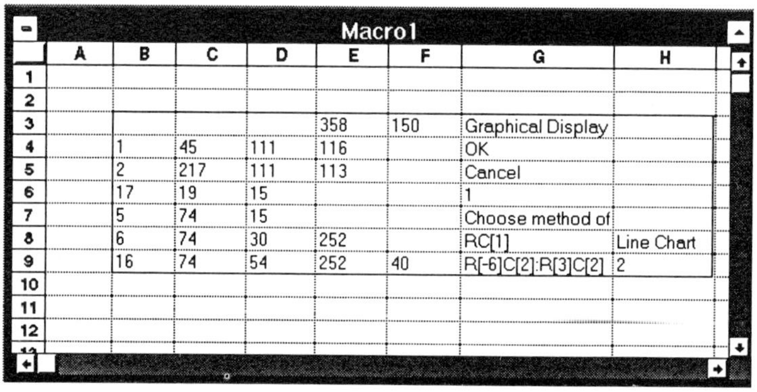

	A	B	C	D	E	F	G	H
1								
2								
3					358	150	Graphical Display	
4		1	45	111	116		OK	
5		2	217	111	113		Cancel	
6		17	19	15			1	
7		5	74	15			Choose method of	
8		6	74	30	252		RC[1]	Line Chart
9		16	74	54	252	40	R[-6]C[2]:R[3]C[2]	2
10								
11								
12								

(Window title: Macro1)

Figure 11.5 Excel Macro sheet showing Dialog Box information in cells B3:H9.

Dialog Box Definitions

The definition of the dialog box has the following layout :

Column 1: This is the Item number. An example would be 12, representing an option button.

Column 2: The X-position of the item's upper-left corner.

Column 3: The Y-position of the item's upper-left corner.

Column 4:   Screen width of the item.

Column 5:   Screen height of the item.

These five properties are all automatically provided by the dialog editor when the image is pasted into an Excel worksheet. Normally these should not be changed manually, although it can be done.

Column 6:   This is the text associated with the item. This field can either be actual text or, as in the case of a list box, can be a reference to a range of cells that contains the items, i.e. text options, for the list box. The reference to the cells containing the items which will be used by the list box must be in an R1C1 format i.e. not, for example, G7:G12. This is done by temporarily switching to R1C1 format by selecting the Workspace option of the Options menu and then clicking on the R1C1 checkbox.

Column 7:   This is the initial value or result value for the item. For example, in the case of a check box item, a value of TRUE in this column would indicate that the check box is initially turned on, and conversely a value of FALSE would indicate that the box is off.

In order to display the dialog box, a macro needs to be created which uses the definition that has just been pasted into the macro sheet. The function to display a dialog box is:

```
=DIALOG.BOX(cell_range)
```

where cell_range is the area covered by the entire dialog data in the macro sheet, e.g. (E4:K11). (Note: the dialog occupies 7 columns and 1 row for each item in the dialog box, plus an extra row at the top of the definition for the dialog box itself.)

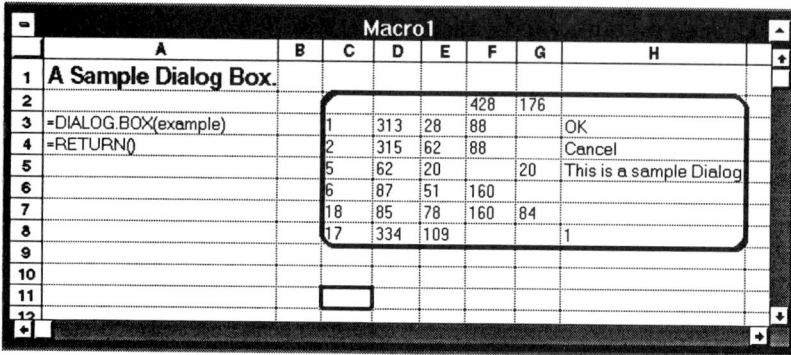

Figure 11.6 Sample macro sheet containing dialog.box function call.

The cell_range parameter can also be a text name, as shown in figure 11.6, which represents the region covered by the dialog box definition. To do this, select the area covered by the dialog box definition and then select Define Name from the Formula menu option. The area range will be displayed in the Refers to box. You should type in a name for the area into the Name box as shown in figure 11.7.

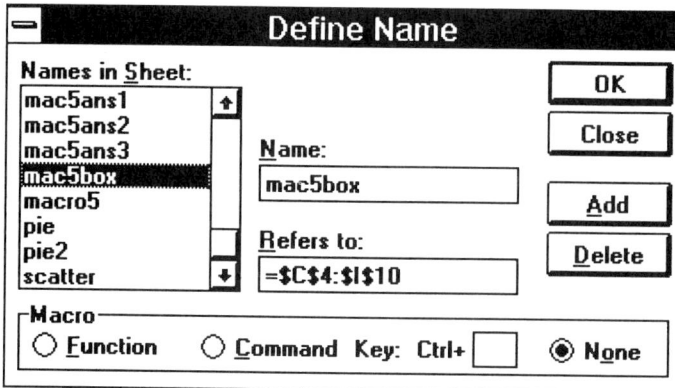

Figure 11.7 Defining a name for a dialog box definition.

Do not select the Command option button at this point as this is used for defining names for entire macro sheets and subroutines. Select OK to define.

Running the macro sheet that contains this function will display the dialog box.

If the dialog box has push buttons, such as Cancel, then to determine which button was pressed and hence take the relevant action required by the macro, all that needs to be done is examine the value of the cell which contains the =DIALOG.BOX() function since a dialog box automatically returns the value of the button selected to this cell. As an example: if the =DIALOG.BOX() is located in cell A7, then after the dialog has been executed the return value will be placed in cell A7. If the Cancel button was pressed, then cell A7 will have the value FALSE. If another button in the box was selected and, as an example, that was the second item in the dialog box definition, then the value of cell A7 will be 2.

One error that can occur when defining the =DIALOG.BOX() function is that Excel will display an error message stating that 'Function is not valid'. The most common reason for this is that the sheet is not a macro sheet but a worksheet. Only a macro sheet can be used for functions such as =DIALOG.BOX(). An obvious indicator of what type of sheet is being used is the suffix to the sheet's name, for instance .XLS for a worksheet and .XLM for a macro sheet. If there is no extension at the current time and the name of the sheet is not obviously MACRO1 or SHEET1, then one method of determining which sheet is being used is to overfill a cell with letters, eg. aaaaa. A worksheet cell will overspill into the next cell whereas a macro sheet will not.

This ease of use makes dialog boxes an attractive proposition when developing simple Excel applications.

Documenting Macros

As with all programs, it is good practice to put comments in macros to aid understanding in the future - both for the writer and others who may need to maintain or look at the macro. With Excel version 3.0, it is possible to really 'go to town' with this documentation and we would encourage budding macro writers to do so and follow some of the guidelines in this section.

First of all we suggest that users place all code, dialog boxes and variable work areas in the same places within their macro sheets. A good example would be: column A for the main macro code, column B for subroutine macros, column C for the start of Dialog Box definitions, and so on.

This common 'look and feel' for macro sheets, either within an organisation or from one developer, will help enormously in both creating new macros and maintaining older ones.

You should also use the Excel drawing tools found on the toolbar to highlight areas of specific interest on the macro sheet. This combined with a good (and standard) use of colour is an excellent documentation aid. Again, as an example, drawing a bright red box around the main macro code and then drawing an arrow pointing to this box with a message such as 'main macro code' to label it, will help explain to inexperienced macro users what is where.

Remember also that with Excel, comments can go anywhere within a command macro. This is because Excel skips over any cells containing text, that is those not beginning with an '=' sign (which normally designates that an Excel formula is to follow). Therefore, comments and named cells can be placed anywhere within the macro code without affecting the way the macro runs. This is especially useful if adjacent columns to the code are not available to put notes and comments in; perhaps they contain subroutine macros or dialog box definitions.

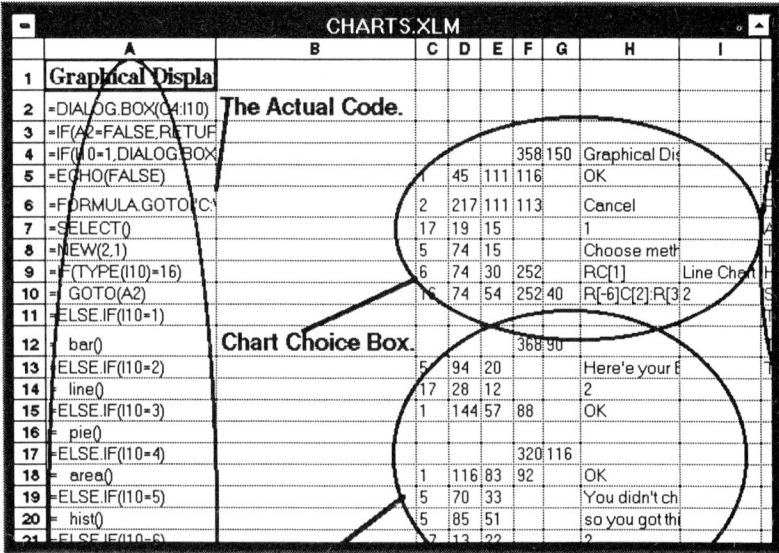

	A	B	C	D	E	F	G	H	I
1	Graphical Displa								
2	=DIALOG.BOX(Q4:I10)	The Actual Code.							
3	=IF(A2=FALSE,RETUF								
4	=IF(I10=1,DIALOG.BOX						358	150 Graphical Dis	
5	=ECHO(FALSE)			45	111	116		OK	
6	=FORMULA.GOTO('C:\		2	217	111	113		Cancel	
7	=SELECT()		17	19	15			1	
8	=NEW(2,1)		5	74	15			Choose meth	
9	=F(TYPE(I10)=16)		6	74	30	252		RC[1]	Line Cha
10	= GOTO(A2)			74	54	252	40	R[-6]C[2]:R[3 2	
11	ELSE.IF(I10=1)								
12	bar()	Chart Choice Box.					368 90		
13	ELSE.IF(I10=2)		5	94	20			Here'e your E	
14	line()		17	28	12			2	
15	ELSE.IF(I10=3)		1	144	57	88		OK	
16	pie()								
17	ELSE.IF(I10=4)						320 116		
18	area()		1	116	83	92		OK	
19	ELSE.IF(I10=5)		5	70	33			You didn't ch	
20	hist()		5	85	51			so you got thi	
21	ELSE.IF(I10=6)		7	13	22			2	

Figure 11.8 Documenting and laying out a macro makes it understandable.

Q+E

Q+E (pronounced Q plus E or, more commonly, Q and E) is a software product built by Pioneer Software Systems. It is currently supplied free of charge with copies of Excel 3.0 for Windows. It is designed to allow users to manipulate and update various database files - even from within an Excel spreadsheet. It currently supports a large number of database files on a number of database systems. Examples are dBASE, Microsoft SQL Server and IBM's OS/2 Extended Edition Database Manager, to name but a few. The Q+E main menu is shown in figure 11.9.

With Q+E: the ability exists for users to open several database files simultaneously and copy data from one database and insert it into another; data can be copied from a database via Q+E and then inserted into applications, such as Excel. This could then be used to, say, create graphical representations of this data. Data that is copied to applications such as Excel can also be automatically updated if the residual database alters, by using the DDE (Dynamic Data Exchange) facilities of Windows.

Q+E allows records, which have been retrieved into a Q+E window from a database such as SQL Server, to be queried in order to obtain more specific information and data from the database files. This query can be done using the generous menu options available within Q+E, or using SQL (Structured Query Language) which is the common language used to access, update and modify relational databases.

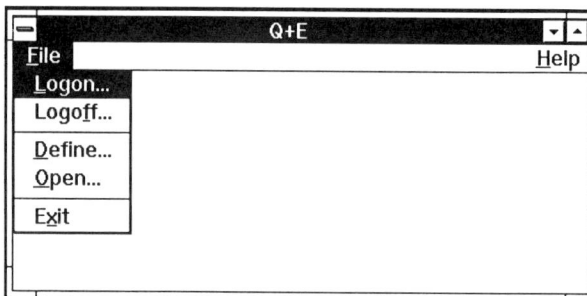

Figure 11.9 Q+E main window.

The menu options of Q+E allow users to sort, format and select individual records. Calculations, such as totalling columns, can also be performed.

The edit facilities of Q+E allow users to dynamically update fields in a remote database. For example, this could involve a database residing on SQL Server on another machine across a network. This is done using the paste link facility. Effectively this means that whenever a user changes a value in the table that is currently in a

Q+E window, such as updating or even deleting a value, then that change is broadcasted to the database server which actually makes the same changes to the data. This is, perhaps, the most powerful feature of Q+E since it allows simple front-end applications to be developed in Excel which can automatically link to the required data on a remote server, can extract that data into an Excel spreadsheet, and then allow a spreadsheet user to do whatever they want with that data - perhaps even graph it!

VISUAL BASIC

Microsoft Visual Basic is a product that allows novice and experienced users alike to quickly and easily build powerful full-featured Windows applications.

Visual Basic takes total control over the development of your application and ensures that programming is minimised so that the developer is then able to concentrate on the application's user interface and functionality.

Features Supported

Features of Visual Basic include:

o   Everything required to create Windows applications, for example, push buttons, pull down menus, scroll bars, check boxes, list boxes, combo boxes, etc.

o   The ability to show and hide any number of items at run time, including the ability to interact with multiple windows in an application.

o   Communication with other Windows applications through Dynamic Data Exchange (DDE). This is the process of two applications talking to each other by automating the manual process of cutting and pasting data between applications.

o   An extensive icon library that has been designed to cater for all types of applications, coupled with an extremely comprehensive on-line tutorial.

o   Graphical statements, powerful maths and string-handling libraries, easy to use string variables, fixed and dynamic arrays, random-access and sequential file support, and sophisticated run-time error-handling.

o   The incorporation of functions written in another language, and compiled into a Dynamic Link Library. Also, direct access to the Application Programming Interface.

o   The ability to create an executable stand-alone object code version of your application for distribution with a run-time module.

Visual Basic Defined

Once you have installed Visual Basic and double-clicked on its icon, you should be presented with several windows as shown in figure 11.10.

On starting up Visual Basic, four windows are initially scattered across the screen. The bigger screen you have, so the better development environment you will have.

The rather long window at the top, in figure 11.10 contains all of the traditional drop-down menus that enable you to open, save and print as well as the standard editing facilities such as cut, copy, paste and delete. Just below the drop-down menus there is the properties bar.

Every item that you draw, for example, push buttons, text boxes, check boxes, etc, are known as controls and each control has a number of properties. A property for a push button control could be, for example, the text shown on that button, whether it is a default button or the name given to the push button control. There are lots of properties that need to be set at design-time for each control to help make your applications look extremely professional. The properties bar contains two combo boxes: the one on the left contains the names of all the properties for a selected control and the one on the right is used to enter values for each of the properties.

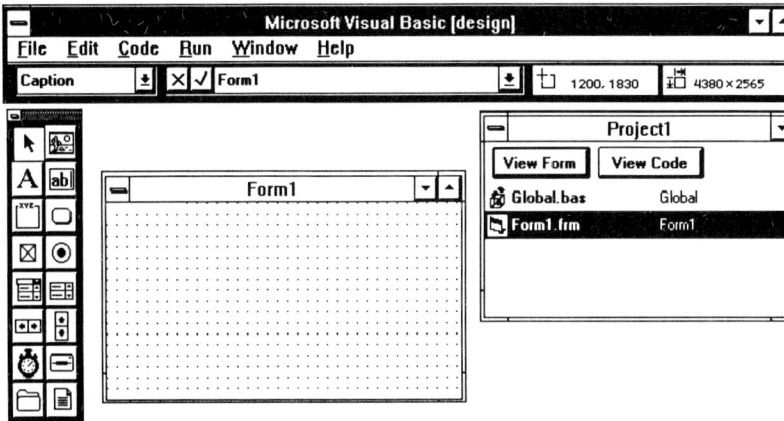

Figure 11.10 Initial Visual Basic Windows.

The window to the left, in figure 11.10 is known as the toolbox. Visual Basic supplies you with 16 different tools (or 16 controls), that you can draw on your window or dialog box, which are collectively known as forms. To actually draw a control on your form, click on the required tool using the mouse and mouse pointer, move over to your form and then again by using the mouse, draw the control. Once you have done this, while you are still in design-mode, you can move the control around and re-size it by just using the mouse.

On the right hand side in figure 11.10 there is a window labelled Project1. This is known as the project window and contains all of the forms that are used for a particular application. For each form you have the ability to view the code or view the form, and thus the project window enables you to manage your application efficiently at design-time.

The window in the centre in figure 11.10, labelled Form1, is your initial form that you can immediately begin working with. It is covered with small dots to indicate that you are in design-mode. This is also a control and as with all controls, has its own set of properties.

It is straightforward to enter code to make your applications work. If you want to do some processing when the user clicks on the OK button for example, then all you have to do is, during design-time, double-click on the OK button and a code template in a window appears on the screen. Now enter the code you want to execute when the user performs this action. You can do this for all of the controls with great ease.

Beginners All-purpose Symbolic Instruction Code

The BASIC part of Visual Basic is a terrific improvement over many BASIC implementations. Gone are the needs for line numbers, excessive use of the goto keyword and dynamically typed variables (although you can still use them). Visual Basic allows global variables, dynamic arrays, the ability to declare variables before you use them, and above all, the ability to modularise your programs.

Visual Basic is incredibly easy to use. Once a few string-handling and file- handling functions are mastered users will be able to quickly develop applications like that shown in figure 11.11. This is a simple application that took only a few hours to develop - allowing users to easily manipulate an on-line company phone-book.

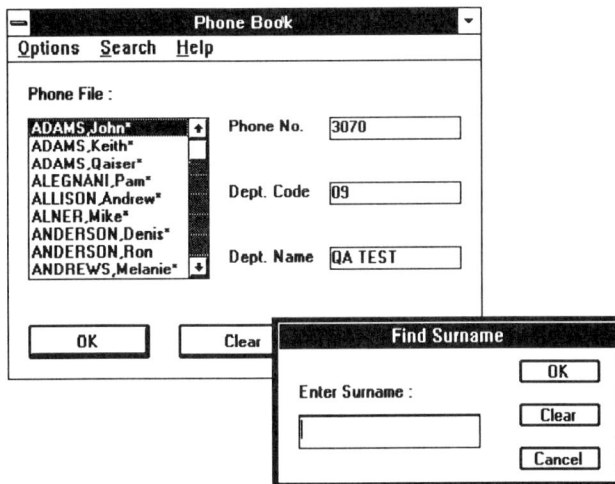

Figure 11.11 A small Phone Book application built with Visual Basic.

Visual Basic enables users to create stand-alone executable files (i.e. a .EXE file). If you distribute your executable files to others you will also need to distribute the supplied Dynamic Link Library (DLL), VBRUN100.DLL. This can be done with no additional licence payments.

Visual Basic uses what is called a threaded p-code incremental compiler. When you create an executable file, Visual Basic does not create machine code but rather an intermediate file format. The file VBRUN100.DLL contains the incremental compiler that gets your executable file ready for execution whenever a user runs it.

Making use of Dynamic Data Exchange

One of the most powerful aspects of Visual Basic is its ability to communicate with other applications. Visual Basic does this in the standard manner by implementing Dynamic Data Exchange.

As we have already discussed, DDE is a mechanism that enables two applications to talk to each other by continuously and automatically exchanging data. It automates the manual cutting and pasting of data between applications, providing a fast method of updating and sharing information.

For two applications to exchange information, a DDE conversation has to be initiated between a client and a server. The client application initiates the conversation and the server application responds to it. The client must specify two things in order to begin a conversation:

(1) The name of the server application it wants to talk to.

(2) The subject of the conversation - called the topic.

For example, to start a conversation between Visual Basic, the client, and Microsoft Excel, the server, the DDE application name would be Excel and the topic would be the name of the file that we wished to communicate with.

To communicate with an Excel spreadsheet via a text box created in Visual Basic (the text box having the control name DdeText), you would need to set the appropriate LinkTopic property as follows:

```
DdeText.LinkTopic = "Excel|c:\excel\example.xls"
```

To specify an item for conversation, for example a cell in the spreadsheet file EXAMPLE.XLS, you would have to set the LinkItem property:

```
DdeText.LinkItem = "R1C1"
```

The R1C1 stands for row 1, column 1 in the spreadsheet mentioned previously. Now that we have specified the application to converse with, the topic for conversation and the item used for conversation, all we have to do is activate the link. This is done by setting the LinkMode property.

By setting the LinkMode property to HOT (1), the link is activated and is maintained until the LinkMode property is set to NONE (2). If you change the value of the LinkTopic property, Visual Basic terminates the old conversation. Therefore, it is good practice to set LinkMode to NONE before changing the LinkTopic property, so that any existing link is terminated before the new one is activated.

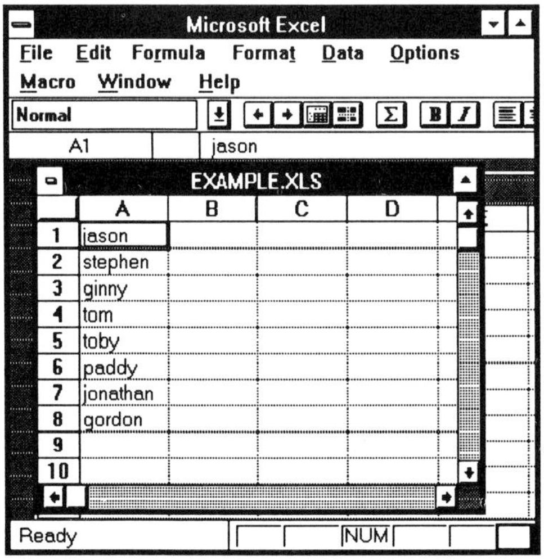

Figure 11.12 Spreadsheet data for our example DDE conversation.

The Technical Guide to Windows

To try out dynamic data exchange, let's build an application in Visual Basic that will communicate with a Microsoft Excel spreadsheet. Enter data in a spreadsheet file, call it EXAMPLE.XLS, as shown in figure 11.12.

The Visual Basic program will copy each cell from the spreadsheet, that contains a name, and paste this data into a text box in the Visual Basic application.

Create the form, shown in figure 11.13, using Visual Basic.

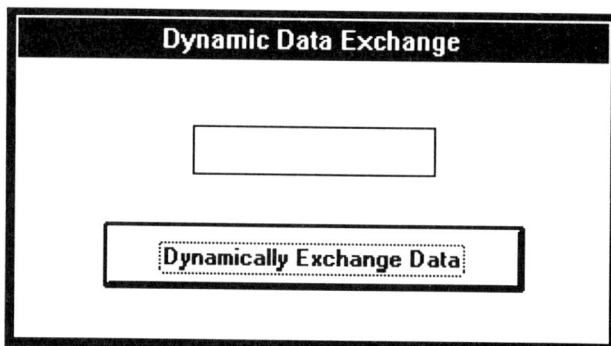

Figure 11.13 The Dialog Box used to demonstrate DDE.

The CtlName for the text box should be DDEText and the CtlName for the Button should be DDEButton. The code needed is shown in figure 11.14.

```
Sub DDEButton_Click ()

        Const HOT  = 1
        Const NONE = 0
        Static Row As Integer
        Row = Row + 1
        If (Row = 1) Or (Row = 9) Then
              Row =1
              DDEText.LinkMode  = NONE
              DDEText.LinkTopic = "Excel|c:\excel\example.xls"
              DDEText.LinkItem  = "R1C1"
```

```
        DDEText.LinkMode  = HOT
    Else
        DDEText.LinkItem  = "R" + LTrim$(Str$(Row)) + "C1"
    End If

End Sub
```

Figure 11.14 Code that copies data from one application and pastes it into another.

Notice the use of the LinkMode, LinkTopic and LinkItem properties in figure 11.14 that we discussed previously.

Every time you click the button in your Visual Basic application, the (next) name in the column in the Excel spreadsheet will be pasted into your Visual Basic application. Once the last name is pasted, it will start pasting from the beginning again.

Obviously, using this feature of Visual Basic and building dialogs with Excel, quite sophisticated application systems can easily be created.

Using Other Languages

Visual Basic allows the calling of functions written in other languages. For example, sophisticated developers may wish to build applications or standard bits of code in C and then bundle that code into a Dynamic Link Library (DLL). Once you have or are supplied with a function in DLL format you will be able call functions declared in the DLL from your Visual Basic programs. This ability now gives you much more power than you originally had with just Visual Basic. Remember, Visual Basic allows you to do everything that the C language makes very complicated, for example the creation of the user interface and the handling of events. C does however allow you to do many things that Visual Basic cannot, for example accessing networked database files or doing things at the operating system level.

If you or support people in your organisation bundle C code into DLLs and you access them from within Visual Basic you have a very powerful system at your disposal, as long as you can call the DLL routines and return from them without error.

As an example, if the DLL is located in the root directory of your PC and is called MYLIB.DLL, then to access a function within the DLL called HI, you will need to make the following declaration in the Global module or in the module that will make the call to the DLL :

```
Declare Function HI Lib "C:\MYLIB.DLL" (ByVal a%) As Integer
```

This means that HI is a function in which only one integer value has to be passed (this is specified by ByVal a%), and it returns an integer value. To use this function, all you have to do is call it as you would any Visual Basic function, for example :

```
ReturnValue% = HI(13)
```

With Visual Basic, you can call other files in other formats, for example, .EXE files, and execute these directly via the Visual Basic Shell function command. If we had a normal Windows application called WINHELLO.EXE it could be executed as follows:

```
ReturnValue% = Shell("c:\winhello.exe",1)
```

Dynamic Windows

Window controls (such as icons, buttons, pull-down options etc.) can be manipulated at run-time using Visual Basic. This allows a user to disable them (i.e. grey them out), rename their captions or change their size - a very professional touch in any Windows applications that you create.

To do this, all you have to do is set the relevant properties for a control. Remember it is useful to have the ability to enable and disable pull-down menu options and push buttons during run-time so that users do not choose some action that is inappropriate at a point in time.

Figure 11.15 shows the code behind a window (Form_Load) that shows how the size of a window can be changed at run-time.

```
Sub Form_Load ()

        XCoord% = 3960
        YCoord% = 2940
        WindowWidth% = 1550
        WindowHeight% = 1250
        Form1.Show
        MyStep1% = 200
        MyStep2% = 400
        UpperLimit% = 5550
        LowerLimit% = 1550
        Limit% = UpperLimit%

        For ThisLoop% = 1 To 10

                Do Until (WindowWidth% = Limit%)

                        Form1.Move XCoord%, YCoord%,
                            WindowWidth%, WindowHeight%
                        WindowWidth% = WindowWidth% + MyStep2%
                        WindowHeight% = WindowHeight% + MyStep2%
                        XCoord% = XCoord% - MyStep1%
                        YCoord% = YCoord% - MyStep1%

                Loop

                MyStep1% = -(MyStep1%)
                MyStep2% = -(MyStep2%)

                If (Limit% = UpperLimit%) Then
                        Limit% = LowerLimit%
                Else
                        Limit% = UpperLimit%
                End If

        Next ThisLoop%

End Sub
```

Figure 11.15 Code that demonstrates how dynamic windows can be implemented.

If you try out this code, you will see what sort of impressive graphical effects can easily be created.

Accessing Windows APIs

Visual Basic allows users to make direct calls to the Windows APIs (Application Programming Interfaces). This is as simple as declaring and calling a function stored in a DLL, as previously described. Really impressive results can easily be obtained using these APIs if you just take the time to learn the correct calls and to experiment a little with each API.

However, if you are planning to play around with the Windows APIs we strongly suggest that you get hold of the ASCII file, WINAPI.TXT. This is supplied free of charge by Microsoft and can be found on Compuserve (and probably other bulletin boards). It can save the Visual Basic programmer a lot of time as it contains the correct declarations for all Windows 3 API function calls. Figure 11.16 shows the first few lines of WINAPI.TXT.

```
'  ---------------------------------------------------------'
'
'     WINAPI.TXT -- Windows 3.0 API Declarations for Visual Basic
'
'            Copyright (C) 1991 Microsoft Corporation
'
'  You have a royalty-free right to use, modify, reproduce and distribute
'  this file (and/or any modified version) in any way you find useful,
'  provided that you agree that Microsoft has no warranty, obligation or
'  liability for its contents.  Refer to the Microsoft Windows Programmer's
'  Reference for further information.
'
'  ---------------------------------------------------------

'   General Purpose Defines

Global Const NULL = 0

Type RECT
        left As Integer
        top As Integer
        right As Integer
```

```
        bottom As Integer
End Type

Type POINTAPI
        x As Integer
        y As Integer
End Type

'  ----------------------------------------------------------
'   Kernel Section
'  ----------------------------------------------------------

' ParameterBlock description structure for use with LoadModule
Type PARAMETERBLOCK
        wEnvSeg As Integer
        lpCmdLine As Long
        lpCmdShow As Long
        dwReserved As Long
End Type

'  Loader Routines
Declare Function GetVersion Lib "Kernel" () As Integer
Declare Function GetNumTasks Lib "Kernel" () As Integer
...
```

Figure 11.16 The very first few lines of WINAPI.TXT.

Through the remainder of this chapter we will take a look at some simple uses of using Windows API calls from Visual Basic.

Stretching Icons

As an example, let's look at an application where you need to take a bitmap or an icon and stretch or shrink it so that it fits inside a fixed sized window or picture box.

To do this you must make a call to the GDI function called StretchBlt. To make a call to an API, you must first determine which library it is in, which will be either User, Kernel or GDI. Once you have done this, you must declare it. This can be done by inserting the following statement in the Global module:

```
Declare Function StretchBlt Lib "GDI"
        (ByVal a%, ByVal b%, ByVal c%, ByVal d%,
```

```
             ByVal e%, ByVal f%, ByVal g%, ByVal h%,
                ByVal i%, ByVal j%, ByVal k&)
```

As you can see, this function must receive eleven parameters. As an example of using this API, create a form which has one push button and three picture boxes (small, medium and large) and set their properties as follows:

CONTROL	CTLNAME	WIDTH	HEIGHT
Push Button	Command1	[anything]	[anything]
Small Picture Box	Picture1	495	495
Middle Picture Box	Picture2	1095	1095
Large Picture Box	Picture3	1935	1935

Load an icon into the small picture box (you can use any of the icons stored in the icon library supplied with Visual Basic or one of your own). Set the Caption property on the push button to Expand. Once you have done this, enter the code shown in figure 11.17 behind the Expand push button.

```
Sub Command1_Click()

    Pic1% = Picture1.hDC
    Pic2% = Picture2.hDC
    Pic3% = Picture3.hDC
    ReturnValue% = StretchBlt(Pic2%,0,0,Picture2.Width,
        Picture2.Height,Pic1%,0,0,480,480,&HCC0020)
    ReturnValue% = StretchBlt(Pic3%,0,0,Picture3.Width,
        Picture3.Height,Pic1%,0,0,480,480,&HCC0020)

End Sub
```

Figure 11.17 StretchBlt code behind the expand button.

Once you have done this, run the application, click on the Expand push button, and see what happens!

The Professional About Box

An ABOUT box like that shown in figure 11.18, with information on the current Windows mode, the microprocessor type (CPU), the presence or not of a Math coprocessor (MCP) and the amount of free memory available gives that finishing and professional touch to Windows applications - including those that you build with Visual Basic.

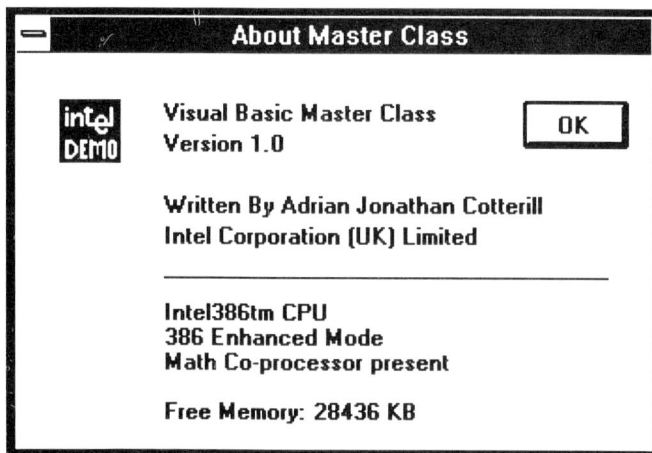

Figure 11.18 An example ABOUT box built using Visual Basic.

Determining the CPU/MCP combination with Visual Basic is a simple task of calling the GetWinFlags Windows API, requiring two bits of code: the appropriate declarations and constants shown in figure 11.19 and the logic shown in figure 11.20.

In figure 11.19, we declare the GetWinFlags API as a function and the appropriate constants needed, with the relevant values obtained either from the Windows Software Developer's Kit reference manual or from the WINAPI.TXT file.

The Technical Guide to Windows

```
Declare Function GetWinFlags Lib "kernel" () As Long
Declare Function GetFreeSpace Lib "kernel" (ByVal wFlags%) As Long

Const WF_STANDARD = &H10
Const WF_ENHANCED = &H20
Const WF_80x87 = &H400

Const WF_PMODE = &H1

Const WF_CPU486 = &H8
Const WF_CPU386 = &H4
Const WF_CPU286 = &H2

Const WF_WIN286 = &H10
Const WF_WIN386 = &H20
Const WF_LARGEFRAME = &H100
Const WF_SMALLFRAME = &H200
```

Figure 11.19 Visual Basic decalarations - in object (general)

The code shown in figure 11.20 calls the GetWinFlags API and then evaluates the result to determine the CPU/MCP combination and Windows modes.

```
Dim CRLF As String
Dim Processor As String
Dim Mode As String
Dim CoProcessor As String

WinFlags = GetWinFlags()

CRLF = Chr$(13) + Chr$(10)

If WinFlags And WF_CPU486 Then
     Processor = "Intel486DX CPU or Intel487SX Math CoProcessor"
ElseIf WinFlags And WF_CPU386 Then Processor = "Intel386tm CPU"
     Else Processor = "Intel286tm CPU"
End If

If WinFlags And WF_ENHANCED Then
     Mode = "386 Enhanced Mode"
Else Mode = "Standard Mode"
End If

If WinFlags And WF_80x87 Then
     CoProcessor = "Present"
ElseIf WinFlags And WF_CPU486 Then
     Processor = "Intel486tm SX CPU"
     CoProcessor = "None"
```

```
End If

' Display configuration values in Lbl_Info.Caption
' (NOTE: CRLF variable causes a line break in a labels caption)
'

Lbl_Info.Caption = Processor + CRLF + Mode + CRLF + "Math Co-processor: "
      + CoProcessor + CRLF + CRLF + "Free Memory: "
      + Format$(GetFreeSpace(0) \ 1024) + " KB"
```

Figure 11.20 Visual Basic Code for CPU/MCP Detection

The important point to note in the code in figure 11.20 is that when we test the WF_CPU486 flag and find it to be true we only know roughly, that the system contains some sort of Intel486 CPU or math coprocessor. So in this example code we initialise an appropriate string variable (called Processor) to contain "Intel486tm DX CPU or Intel487tm SX Math Coprocessor".

Not until we have tested the WF_80x87 flag will we know if the i486 CPU or Math Coprocessor is really an Intel486 SX CPU (see Appendix A for more information about the differences between the Intel486 DX and SX CPUs). Therefore if the WF_80x87 flag tells us that there is no floating point unit on board our i486 processor we override our original diagnosis that the system contained an i486 CPU or i487 SX Math Coprocessor and set the variable (Processor) to "Intel486tm SX CPU".

At the end of the code in figure 11.20, we place the relevant variables in a variable so that they can be displayed in a window.

Note that we also use the Windows GetFreeSpace API in order to show the amount of free memory currently available in the system.

CHAPTER

12

BANYAN VINES

This chapter discusses the running of Windows on client PCs in a Banyan VINES network and describes the procedures that need to be followed in order for Windows and VINES to function together stably. We also discuss some of the Windows 3 functions that can aid your use of VINES and some of the new features of VINES version 4.10.

VINES VERSION 4.00

Support has been provided by Banyan for Windows 3 from version 4.00 of the VINES software. In order to get the two environments to co-exist a patch (VINES patch 1A) needs to be applied to the network server. The patch will have to be installed by the LAN Administrator as only they have the security access required to update the network software. The patch forces the server to shut down during the installation procedure. It is therefore necessary for the work to be carried out during scheduled server down-time.

Once installed, the patch is transparent to non-Windows 3 users and does *not* require them to NEWREV the VINES software held locally on their PC.

Also supplied on the server patch disk is a terminate and stay resident (TSR) routine which needs to be distributed to each LAN workstation which will be using Windows and VINES. TSR2A has to be loaded *after* the network driver program (BAN.EXE) as shown in the example AUTOEXEC.BAT file in figure 12.1, otherwise unpredictable results would occur when using the network.

```
PATH=C:\DOS;C:\BATS;C:\WINDOWS;C:\VINES
KEYB UK
PROMPT $P$G
SET TEMP=C:\WINDOWS\TEMP
CD C:\VINES
BAN /NL
TSR2A
Z:LOGIN
C:
CD C:\
WIN
```

Figure 12.1 Sample AUTOEXEC.BAT file for VINES 4.00 and Windows 3.

Note that in figure 12.1, the /NL switch on the BAN command stops the VINES logon screen from being presented to the user when BAN is loaded. This allows the TSR2A utility to be installed *before* the user logs in and begins work.

VINES VERSION 4.10

Version 4.10 was made available in June 1991 and offers a number of improvements over version 4.00. Of special interest to Windows 3 and OS/2 users is the enhanced support for these environments. The need to install the Windows patch on the server has been removed with VINES 4.10 and the new Windows network driver supplied makes the TSR2A utility redundant. It is now possible to have DOS, Windows and OS/2 clients all co-existing on the same VINES network.

VINES WINDOWS NETWORK DRIVER(S)

Windows 3 provides support for many different networks by means of network drivers. If you look in your SYSTEM.INI file you will see two entries called network.drv - in both the [boot] and [386Enh] sections. If you told Windows that you do not have a network installed your settings would look something like the sample shown in figure 12.2.

```
[boot]
network.drv=

[386Enh]
network.drv=Network not installed
```

Figure 12.2 SYSTEM.INI NETWORK.DRV settings with no network installed.

VINES 4.00, even with the correct patch applied, used the default Microsoft network driver. So if you told Windows SETUP that you were using a Banyan network your SYSTEM.INI file would contain network.drv= entries that pointed to a file called MSNET.DRV. With VINES 4.10, Banyan have supplied their own network driver for use with Windows 3. The new drivers (called VINES.DRV and VVINESD.386) can be found on the Z drive once you have logged on to the network.

Before altering your SYSTEM.INI file make a backup of it, as this will allow you to start again should any problems arise. Edit the SYSTEM.INI file and alter the network.drv to be the same as those in figure 12.3.

```
[boot]
network.drv=vines.drv

[386Enh]
network=*vnetbios, *dosnet, baninst.386
device=vvinesd.386
```

Figure 12.3 SYSTEM.INI NETWORK.DRV settings using VINES 4.10.

Also, if you are upgrading from VINES 4.00 to VINES 4.10 then remember to remove any references to the program TSR2A in any of your batch files as they are no longer needed.

However, rather than making manual changes to Windows system files, installing a network driver is normally a simple matter of choosing the correct network from either the list provided at the hardware selection screen (during installation) or from the SETUP accessory (found in the program group called MAIN).

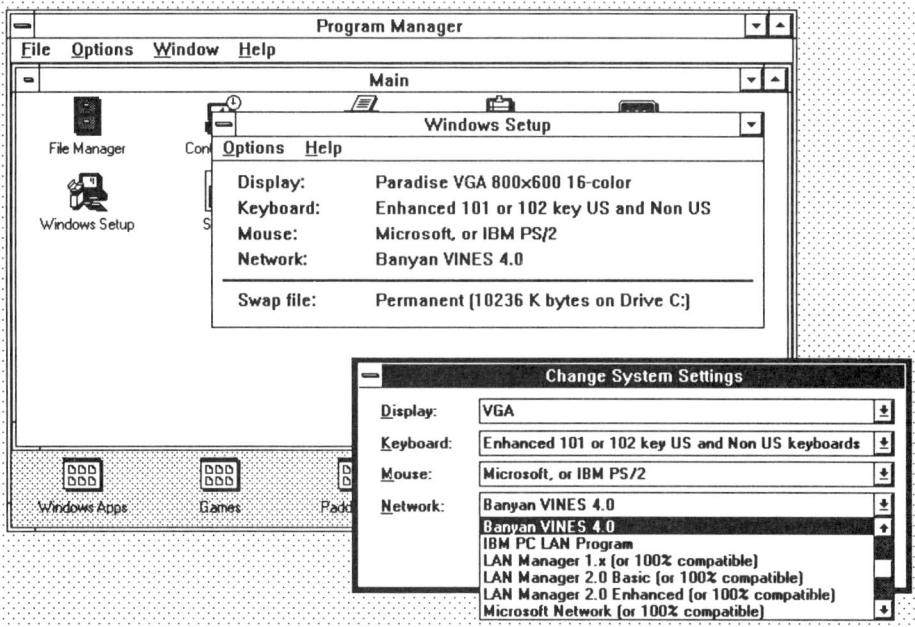

Figure 12.4 Installing the VINES network driver using the SETUP utility.

Windows version 3.0 is not aware of VINES 4.10 and so an option for this new network revision will not appear on the Change System Settings list.

REMOVING HARDWARE INTERRUPT CONFLICTS

One of the great benefits of the IBM PC design is its expandability. However, this flexibility can cause many problems if care is not taken when installing hardware add-ons, e.g. network cards, memory boards, hardcards etc.

INTERRUPT LINE	ASSIGNED TO
00	Timer Output 0
01	Keyboard
02	[Cascade]
03	COM2 (Serial Port 2)
04	COM1 (Serial Port 1)
05	LPT2 (Parallel Port 2)
06	Floppy Disk
07	LPT1 (Parallel Port 1)
08	Real-time Clock
09	Reserved
10	Reserved
11	Reserved
12	Reserved
13	Math Co-processor
14	Fixed Disk
15	Reserved

Figure 12.5 Sample Hardware interrupt assignments of an 80386DX based PC.

PCs designed to the IBM AT standard (most machines containing an Intel 80286 or later processor) are able to support sixteen hardware interrupts. All input/output devices such as hard disks, keyboard, printer and serial ports require an interrupt line to function. If a card is added to a PC which uses an interrupt line already assigned to another device a conflict arises.

Hardware interrupt conflicts can become apparent in a number of ways. Usually the PC becomes erratic with system crashes happening for no apparent reason. A software package such as Norton Utilities or Microsoft's System Diagnostics (MSD) can be used to check the machine for hardware interrupt conflicts.

Once a spare hardware interrupt line has been identified assign the network card to it. The PCCONFIG program in the VINES sub-directory on the workstation can be used to change the interrupt line assignment for the LAN card.

CHANGES TO THE SYSTEM.INI FILE

As we have already seen, when Windows 3 is initially installed a number of files are created which contain parameters that control the way it runs - that is, files in the WINDOWS sub-directory with a INI filename extension.

Most of the settings in these files are chosen automatically by Windows 3 at installation. However, there are three settings that are of interest to the VINES/Windows 3 user. These will now be covered in more detail.

NetHeapSize=kilobytes

This command needs to be added to the [STANDARD] section of the SYSTEM.INI file. It is used to specify the size of a buffer that Windows 3 allocates from conventional memory for the transfer of data over the network. It is only relevant if you are running Windows 3 in standard mode.

Remember, the more memory you allocate to the buffer the less will be available to application programs. There can be no easily recommended figure for the size of the buffer. You will need to experiment to determine the optimum figure for your system.

EMMEXCLUDE=nnnn-nnnn

A number of the devices plugged into a PC, display cards, IRMA cards and LAN cards for example, require memory to use as a communications area. Although the amount of memory required is small, catastrophic effects can occur if it becomes corrupted. It is therefore important that Windows 3 be stopped from trying to use this memory when it is searching for unused address space in RAM.

The EMMEXCLUDE command is used to specify a start and end address of an area of memory that is to be protected from Windows 3. More than one line can be inserted in the [386enh] section to allow for multiple ranges.

The following explains how to exclude the 16K of memory used by a 3Com EtherLink II network card. The process for other cards will be similar: you will need to find the size of the buffer and the address where the buffer is situated in memory.

Run the PCCONFIG program in your VINES sub-directory. Select option 1 (Network Card Settings) and choose the 3Com EtherLink II card from the supplied list. Take a note of the RAM address being used and then return to the DOS prompt by pressing the ESCAPE key three times.

To work out the address range to enter on your EMMEXCLUDE line, add 16K (4000 HEX) to the address you obtained from the Network Card Settings. This can be done with the Windows 3 CALCULATOR in HEX mode,

    e.g.   CC000 + 4000 = D0000 (end address of 16K buffer).

The EMMEXCLUDE line will look like:

```
EMMEXCLUDE=CC00-D000
```

The first digit on the right of each number is dropped. This allows the address range to be rounded to the nearest, whole, 16K block.

InDOSPolling=YES or NO (recommended value: YES)

This command also needs to be inserted in the [386enh] section of the SYSTEM.INI file. When set to YES it prevents Windows 3 from running other applications when memory resident software (e.g. BAN.EXE) has the InDOS flag set on.

INSTALLING THE MS DOS SHARE UTILITY

Microsoft recommend that the MS DOS share utility be installed when running Windows 3 in conjunction with VINES. The SHARE program will ensure that file sharing violations do not occur, or in other words, two applications will be stopped from accessing the same file concurrently.

To load the SHARE program insert the following line in your CONFIG.SYS file. This can be done using the Windows 3 NOTEPAD accessory or DOS' EDLIN.

```
INSTALL=C:\DOS\SHARE.EXE
```

The SHARE program is also required if you are trying to access hard disk partitions larger than 32MB (this is not true if you are using MS-DOS 5.0). It is recommended that *all* VINES users irrespective of whether they are using Windows 3 should install this utility.

THE WINDOWS 3.x FILE MANAGER AND VINES

Banyan VINES uses MS DOS as its interface for communicating with users. You can copy, delete, rename files (access rights permitting) just as though the data was stored locally on your own PC. To allow you to perform these functions when running Windows 3, Microsoft has supplied a utility called the FILE MANAGER. The FILE MANAGER can be found in the program group called MAIN inside the PROGRAM MANAGER. Once run, you are presented with a window containing a graphical representation of the directory structure of the currently selected drive.

Although there are many options for you to use, the two which specifically interest VINES users are CONNECT NET DRIVE and DISCONNECT NET DRIVE. These allow you to access other VINES File Services that are available. For a complete description of the FILE MANAGER read Chapter 4 in the *Microsoft Windows 3 User Guide*.

To connect to VINES File Services, or network drives do the following:

(1) Select the CONNECT NET DRIVE option from the DISK menu.

(2) Select the letter of the drive to be associated with the File Service.

(3) Enter the VINES Street Talk name in the NETWORK PATH box and click on the CONNECT button.

The button marked PREVIOUS allows you to access a list containing all the VINES File Services that you have connected to in the past.

Choose one from the list and click on the SELECT button. This will copy the VINES Street Talk name to the NETWORK PATH box.

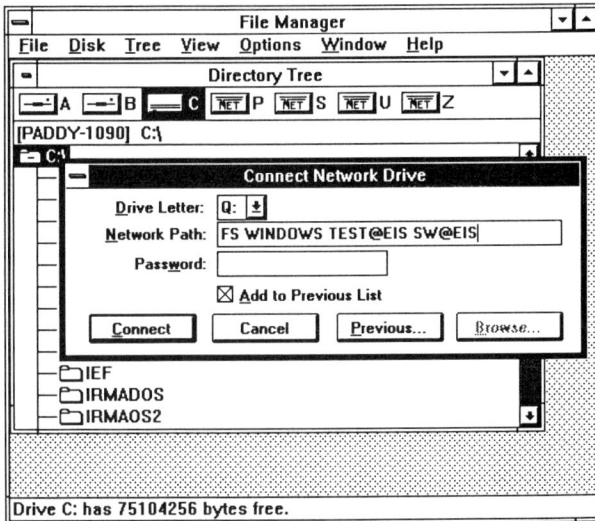

Figure 12.6 Connecting to a VINES File Service.

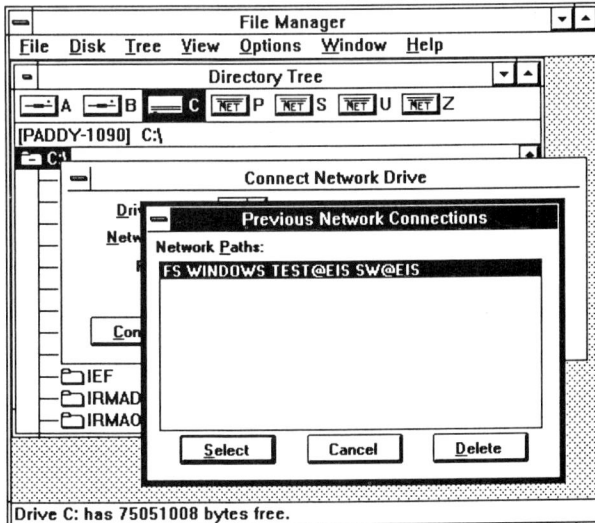

Figure 12.7 List of previously accessed VINES File Services.

When you have finished with a File Service and want to disconnect from it do the following:

(1) Select the DISCONNECT NET DRIVE option from the DISK menu.

(2) Select the letter of the drive to be disconnected and click on the OK button.

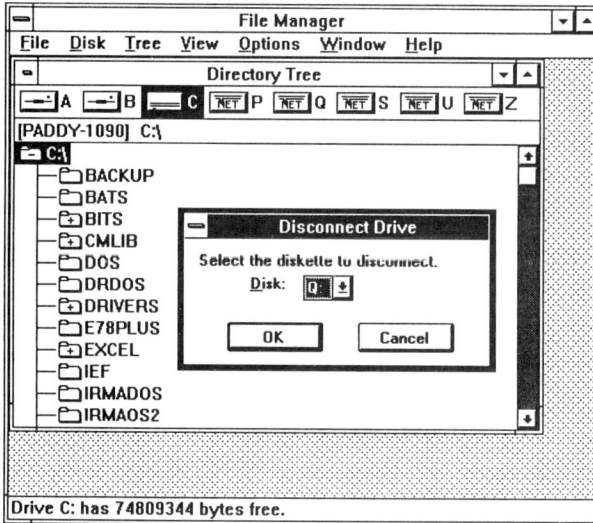

Figure 12.8 Disconnecting from a VINES File Service.

VINES 4.10

The button labelled BROWSE can now be used to list all the currently available file services on the network (see figure 12.9).

```
┌─────────────────────────────────────────────────────────┐
│ ▭                    Browse File Services                 │
├─────────────────────────────────────────────────────────┤
│ StreetTalk: │ File Services      │ ▪ │  Search:          │
│ ┌───────────────────────────────────────────────────┐ ▲▶│
│ │admin Shared Files@admin@png4b                    , │ ▲ │
│ │admin Shared Files@admin@png5a                      │ ▲ │
│ │admin Shared Files@admin@png6a                      │ ▲ │
│ │admin Shared Files@admin@png6b                      │ ▼ │
│ │ADMIN4 Shared Files@ADMIN4@PG4                      │ ▼ │
│ │AIRS@PROD MKTG3 SC@MCG SMD                          │ ▼ │
│ │anywhere@SST OR@ASD                                 │   │
│ └───────────────────────────────────────────────────┘   │
│ Description: General File Service for users in group admin│
│ ┌────────┐  ┌────────┐  ┌────────┐  ┌──────────┐         │
│ │   OK   │  │ Cancel │  │  Help  │  │ Subset...│         │
│ └────────┘  └────────┘  └────────┘  └──────────┘         │
└─────────────────────────────────────────────────────────┘
```

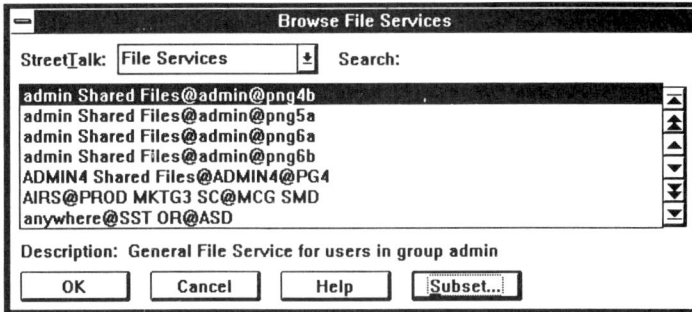

Figure 12.9 VINES 4.10 Browse File Services dialog box.

From the Browse File Services dialog box you can either scroll through the list and select the desired service or narrow the search through the use of the SUBSET option. SUBSET displays another dialog box where it is possible to enter a StreetTalk naming pattern (e.g. *@SALES@COMPANY) and/or a description pattern.

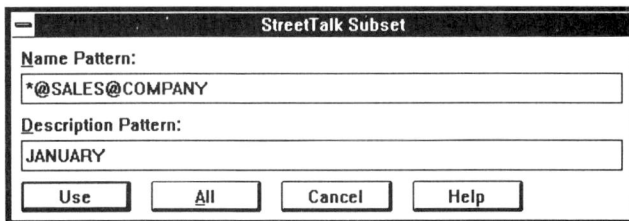

```
┌─────────────────────────────────────────────────────────┐
│ ▭                    StreetTalk Subset                    │
├─────────────────────────────────────────────────────────┤
│ Name Pattern:                                             │
│ ┌───────────────────────────────────────────────────┐   │
│ │*@SALES@COMPANY                                      │   │
│ └───────────────────────────────────────────────────┘   │
│ Description Pattern:                                      │
│ ┌───────────────────────────────────────────────────┐   │
│ │JANUARY                                              │   │
│ └───────────────────────────────────────────────────┘   │
│ ┌────────┐  ┌────────┐  ┌────────┐  ┌────────┐           │
│ │  Use   │  │  All   │  │ Cancel │  │  Help  │           │
│ └────────┘  └────────┘  └────────┘  └────────┘           │
└─────────────────────────────────────────────────────────┘
```

Figure 12.10 VINES 4.10 StreetTalk Subset dialog box.

Once you have entered your desired patterns click on the USE button to display the results. The button labelled ALL can be used to reset the list to the contents of the original, i.e. ALL of the available file services.

From the result list produced by your query select a file service and click on the CONNECT button. As with VINES under DOS it is possible to set the root to be a sub-directory on the network drive. Figure 12.11 shows the dialog box presented to allow this.

```
┌────────────────────────────────────────────────────────┐
│ ▬             Connection Root                           │
├────────────────────────────────────────────────────────┤
│ Root for FS SHARED FILES@EIS SW@EIS [D:]                 │
│ ┌──────────────────────────────────────────────────────┐│
│ │▯                                                      ││
│ └──────────────────────────────────────────────────────┘│
│  ┌───────────┐ ┌───────────┐ ┌───────────┐ ┌──────────┐ │
│  │    OK     │ │   Help    │ │  Cancel   │ │ Browse...│ │
│  └───────────┘ └───────────┘ └───────────┘ └──────────┘ │
└────────────────────────────────────────────────────────┘
```

Figure 12.11 VINES 4.10 Connection to Root dialog box.

As you can probably guess by now the button labelled BROWSE will provide you with a list of all the sub-directories on the network drive, from which you can choose one.

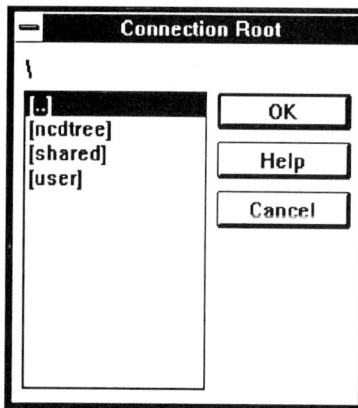

```
┌──────────────────────────────────┐
│ ▬          Connection Root        │
├──────────────────────────────────┤
│  \                                │
│  ┌──────────┐   ┌──────────────┐  │
│  │[▪]       │   │      OK       │ │
│  │[ncdtree] │   └──────────────┘  │
│  │[shared]  │   ┌──────────────┐  │
│  │[user]    │   │     Help      │ │
│  │          │   └──────────────┘  │
│  │          │   ┌──────────────┐  │
│  │          │   │    Cancel     │ │
│  │          │   └──────────────┘  │
│  │          │                     │
│  └──────────┘                     │
└──────────────────────────────────┘
```

Figure 12.12 VINES 4.10 Root Directory selection dialog box.

LOGGING IN AND OUT FROM THE DOS PROMPT

A very useful feature, if you access a number of servers or you are a LAN Administrator, is to be able to log in and out of the network whilst Windows 3 is running. This is possible if you are running Windows 3 in 386 Enhanced mode. Set up an MS DOS session that executes in a window: this session can then be kept active, as an icon on your desktop, until it is needed.

```
┌────────────────────────────── MS DOS 4.01 ──────────────────── ▼ ▲ ┐
│                                                                     │
│ Microsoft(R) MS-DOS(R) Version 4.01                                 │
│            (C)Copyright Microsoft Corp 1981-1988                    │
│                                                                     │
│ C:\> LOGOUT                                                         │
│                                                                     │
│ Come back soon...                                                   │
│                                                                     │
│ C:\> LOGIN                                                          │
│                                                                     │
│                                                                     │
│                                                                     │
│                                                                     │
│                                                                     │
│                                                                     │
│                                                                     │
│                                                                     │
└─────────────────────────────────────────────────────────────────────┘
```

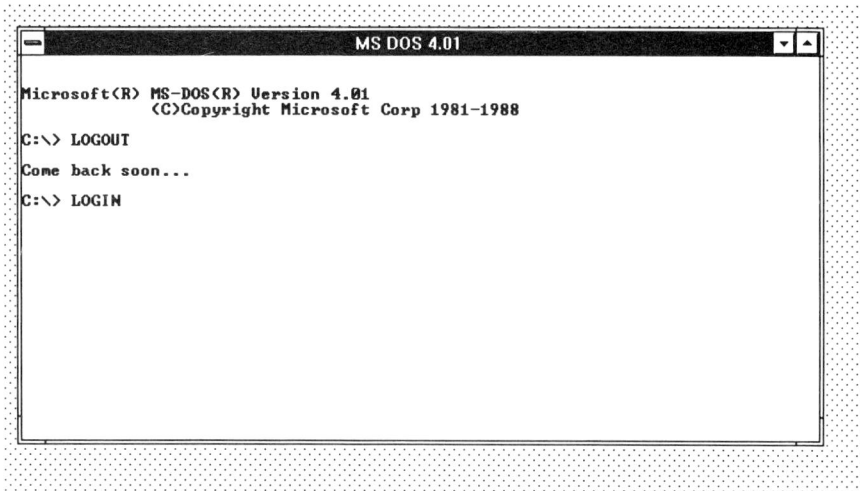

Figure 12.13 Logging out and in of the network from a windowed DOS session.

VINES 4.10

The ability to log in and out of VINES from the Window DOS prompt has been removed. If you attempt to logout from the DOS prompt the message 'Please exit Windows before running LOGOUT' will be displayed.

INSTALLING NETWORK PRINTERS

The process for using printers on your VINES network under Windows 3 is almost the same as for a printer attached locally to your PC. The first stage is to run the PRINTERS utility in the CONTROL PANEL, which is in the program group called MAIN.

Click on the ADD PRINTER button and select your printer from the list provided. Windows 3 will check to see if the printer driver is already on your hard disk; if not it will ask you to insert the Windows 3 disk containing the driver program and load it.

Once you have assigned a printer port, usually LPT1 or LPT2, and set the correct options, return to the PRINTERS dialog box and click on the button marked NETWORK. When you do this you will see the dialog box shown in figure 12.14.

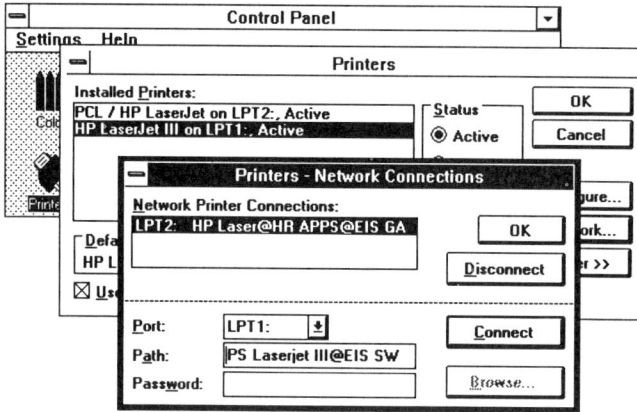

Figure 12.14 Installing a VINES network printer.

In the box labelled PATH enter the VINES Street Talk name of the printer you want to use. If the printer has already been assigned to you via your USER PROFILE the name will be visible in the NETWORK PRINTER CONNECTIONS box.

Select the port you want the VINES printer assigned to and click on the CONNECT button. When using other LAN environments the button labelled BROWSE allows you to view all the printers available for the one you want. Unfortunately this feature does not work with VINES 4.00. The same effect can be achieved using the search facility in the VINES SETPRINT utility.

VINES 4.10

It is now possible via the BROWSE button to view a list of all the print services currently available and to select the one you want.

Figure 12.15 shows the dialog box displayed when the BROWSE option is chosen. As with the File Manager the SUBSET option allows you to search for a particular print service by specifying search parameters.

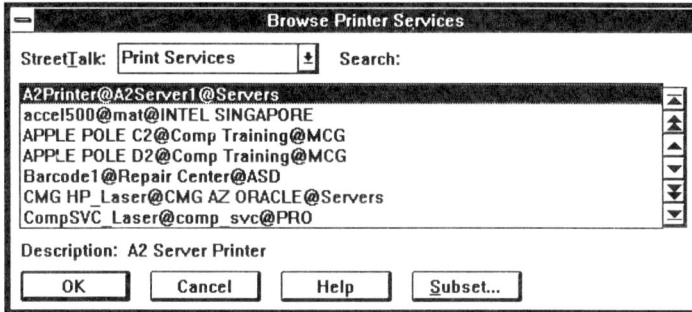

```
┌─────────────────────────────────────────────────────────────┐
│  ─              Browse Printer Services                       │
│  StreetTalk: │Print Services    │ ± │  Search:                │
│  ┌──────────────────────────────────────────────────┬──────┐ │
│  │A2Printer@A2Server1@Servers                         │  ▲   │ │
│  │accel500@mat@INTEL SINGAPORE                        │  ▲   │ │
│  │APPLE POLE C2@Comp Training@MCG                     │  ▶▶▶│ │
│  │APPLE POLE D2@Comp Training@MCG                     │  ▲   │ │
│  │Barcode1@Repair Center@ASD                          │  ▼   │ │
│  │CMG HP_Laser@CMG AZ ORACLE@Servers                  │  ▼   │ │
│  │CompSVC_Laser@comp_svc@PRO                          │  ▼   │ │
│  └──────────────────────────────────────────────────┴──────┘ │
│  Description: A2 Server Printer                               │
│  ┌────────┐  ┌──────────┐  ┌────────┐  ┌──────────┐           │
│  │   OK   │  │  Cancel  │  │  Help  │  │ Subset...│           │
│  └────────┘  └──────────┘  └────────┘  └──────────┘           │
└─────────────────────────────────────────────────────────────┘
```

Figure 12.15 VINES 4.10 Browse print services dialog box.

PRINTING WITH WINDOWS APPLICATIONS

One of the big advantages in using Windows 3 compatible applications is that they are able to take advantage of the Windows 3 print spooler and printer drivers. Printed output is sent as a print file to the PRINT MANAGER and it controls the sending of the information to the printer.

The Windows 3 print spooler is more important to a non-VINES user as VINES provides its own print spooling facility.

PRINTING WITH NON-WINDOWS APPLICATIONS

When printing from a non-Windows 3 application, such as WordPerfect 5.1, the Windows 3 print spooler and printer driver are not used. This means that printing from standard DOS word-processors and spreadsheets may take longer than their Windows 3 compatible counterparts.

MANIPULATING THE PRINT QUEUE

Microsoft Windows 3.0 does not support the displaying and manipulation of VINES 4.00 print queues from the Windows 3 PRINT MANAGER program. If you run the PRINT MANAGER program which is located in the program group called MAIN you will see the screen shown in figure 12.16.

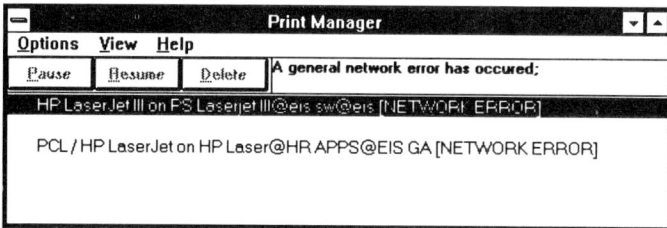

Figure 12.16 Windows 3 PRINT MANAGER.

In the mean time the Banyan utility SETPRINT can be used. Add the SETPRINT program to one of the PROGRAM MANAGER groups. This will allow you to select the program easily and run it as an iconised background task.

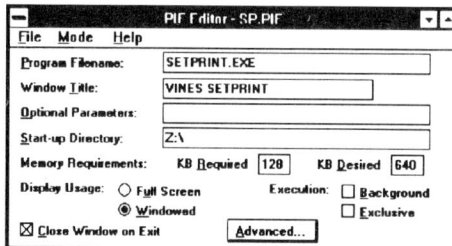

Banyan VINES

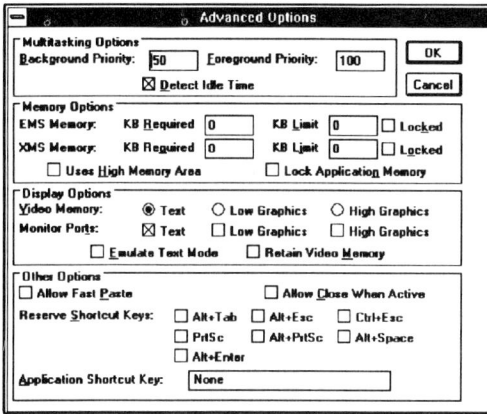

Figure 12.17 Windows 3.0 Program Information File (PIF) for SETPRINT utility.

VINES 4.10

The Print Manager is now able to view VINES print queues and show the jobs currently waiting to print. The functionality is view only and any manipulation of the print queue; job cancelling, reprinting, etc. will still have to be done through the Banyan SETPRINT utility.

To view the jobs currently on a print queue choose SELECTED NET QUEUE from the VIEW menu. The dialog box in figure 12.17 will be shown.

Only the printers (LAN or local) that have been defined to Windows will automatically be displayed in the Print Manager window. To view other VINES print queues select the OTHER NET QUEUE from the VIEW menu and enter the StreetTalk name in the input box. Unfortunately there is no browse option on this dialog box and so it is important to know the exact name of the print service that you want to look at.

- 209 -

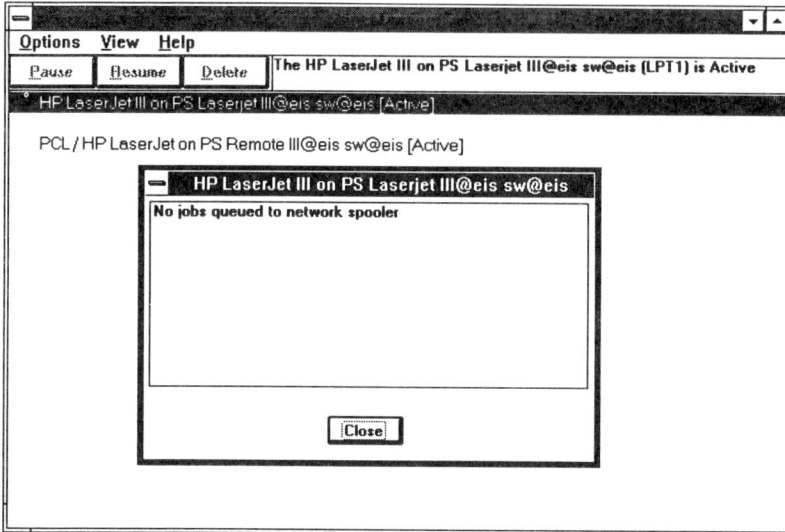

Figure 12.18 Viewing a VINES 4.10 print queue from Print Manager.

IBM 3270 EMULATION

Although users should be careful it is perfectly feasible to run VINES 3270 emulation sessions in a window. However it is possible to suspend the session by using the Windows 3 CUT and PASTE features. This sometimes causes the connection between mainframe, server and PC to be dropped.

The recommended way of running your VINES 3270 session is full screen, from a Windows 3 Program Information File (PIF) which in turn executes a DOS batch (BAT) file. The example files (figures 12.19) can be used as the foundation of your own files.

The placing of a cross in the box labelled PRTSC, in the PIF file, tells Windows 3 if the user requests a screen dump (by pressing the PRINT SCREEN key) to redirect the data to the default printer rather than the Windows 3 CLIPBOARD.

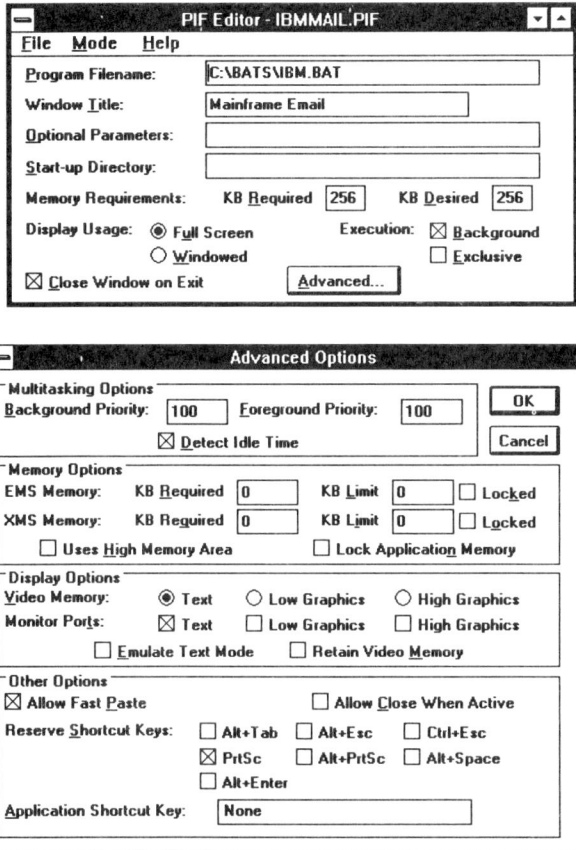

Figure 12.19 Windows 3 Program Information File for VINES 3270 session.

In figure 12.20 a couple of things are of interest. The first is the NUMLUS switch on the R3270 command. This specifies that one 3270 logical unit (LU) should be allocated for this session. The reason for doing this is to reduce memory usage. The default number of LUs for a session is four, with each one requiring 5K of memory. By specifying a value of one, it is possible to save 15K of conventional memory (the first 640K).

```
@ECHO OFF
CLS
Z:\R3270 /NUMLUS:1
Z:\3270 /ADAPTER:C:\VINES\VGA
Z:\REL3270
```

Figure 12.20 MS DOS batch file for running a VINES 3270 session.

The other command of interest is REL3270. This releases the memory being used by the 3270 emulation software when the session is terminated.

Through the use of Windows 3 multi-tasking properties, it is possible to run multiple 3270 sessions concurrently, each one accessing a different facility, e.g. electronic mail and TSO. The number of 3270 sessions that can be run will depend on the amount of memory in your machine, and the other applications that are active.

SETTING NETWORK OPTIONS

Another option called NETWORK is added to the Control Panel if Windows 3 network support has been installed. Depending on the network you are running different options are available.

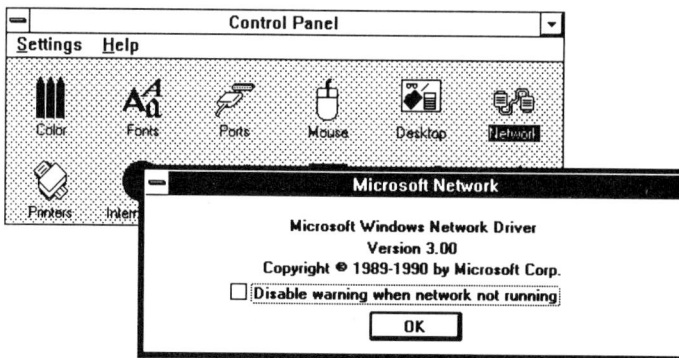

Figure 12.21 Network option dialog box.

Figure 12.21 shows the dialog box which is displayed when support for Banyan VINES 4.00 has been installed. The dialog box will be displayed if you run Windows 3 before you have logged on to the network. Clicking in the box will disable the feature.

VINES 4.10

If you are using VINES 4.10 a different dialog box appears when you click on the NETWORK icon. This can be seen in figure 12.22. The new dialog box also appears when Windows initially loads and provides VINES version information, and the user streetTalk name amongst other data.

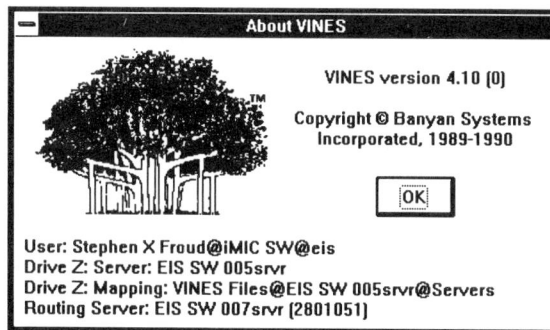

```
━                          About VINES
                                      VINES version 4.10 (0)

                        TM            Copyright © Banyan Systems
                                        Incorporated, 1989-1990

                                             [ OK ]

    User: Stephen X Froud@iMIC SW@eis
    Drive Z: Server: EIS SW 005srvr
    Drive Z: Mapping: VINES Files@EIS SW 005srvr@Servers
    Routing Server: EIS SW 007srvr (2801051)
```

Figure 12.22 VINES 4.10 Network option dialog box.

THE VINES 4.10 MESSAGES APPLICATION

One of the problems when running Windows with VINES 4.00 is the messages that appear on the 25th line of the display. To correct this problem a Windows utility program called MESSAGES is supplied with VINES 4.10 which will pop-up and show you any messages that arrive at your workstation. Figure 12.23 shows an example of the message pop-up dialog box.

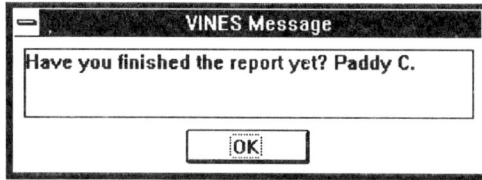

Figure 12.23 VINES 4.10 Message pop-up dialog box.

To start the MESSAGES utility either select RUN from the Program Manager and enter MESSAGES.EXE, or create an icon in one of your program groups with a command line of Z:\MESSAGES.EXE.

If you always logon to the network before running Windows then we would suggest that you edit your WIN.INI file and add Z:\MESSAGES.EXE to the LOAD line at the top. This entry will get Windows to automatically load the MESSAGES program and run it as an icon at the bottom of the screen on startup.

The MESSAGES program can be used to send messages as well as monitoring those that you receive. To create a message select the SEND option on the MESSAGE menu and the SEND dialog box will appear.

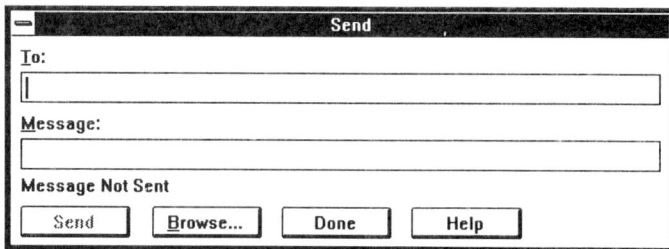

Figure 12.24 SEND dialog box.

There is a BROWSE button which allows you to search for the person to whom you wish to send the message too. As in the File Manager and printer setup the search can be narrowed by supplying a

StreetTalk naming pattern. It is possible to search for users, nicknames and lists.

VINES FUTURES

VINES version 4.10 is a great improvement over VINES 4.00, as it supports both Windows and OS/2 clients. The supporting of OS/2 clients will probably be very important to most organisations currently using VINES as it will allow them to incorporate fast, powerful and flexible database servers, such as, Microsoft SQL Server or ORACLE, into their computing environments.

In the Windows environment VINES 4.10 is much more stable than VINES 4.00 and this is obviously something which will improve further with future software releases; this includes DOS, Windows and VINES itself.

APPENDIX

A

THE COMPUTER INSIDE

The Intel microprocessor is the brain inside every IBM or compatible personal computer, and dictates not only the speed and performance of a desktop computer system but also the kind of software which can be used. The processor in your machine determines the modes that you can run Microsoft Windows in. This appendix discusses the Intel386 range of products and what they mean to users of Microsoft Windows.

A SHORT HISTORY

The very first microprocessor, the Intel 4004, was introduced in 1971, being developed for use in a hand held calculator. It was subsequently adopted for a number of industrial uses (and was even used for controlling traffic lights). The rest of the 1970s saw the development of a number of Intel computer-on-a-chip designs which were later to usher in the PC age.

In 1980, IBM selected the Intel 8088 microprocessor for use in its first personal computer, the IBM PC. This was a milestone in Intel's history and established Intel architecture as the industry standard. Today, more than 80% of the world's desktop computers are based on Intel-designed microprocessors.

16-Bit Computing

Each successive generation of microprocessors has brought corresponding
developments in the software arena. The arrival of the first PCs based on the 16-bit 8086 sparked off the growth of the enormous MS-DOS installed software base.

The massive end-user investment in MS-DOS software, caused Intel to design the 16-bit 80286 microprocessor to be 100% compatible with the 8086/8088, protecting the user's investment in software. A new operating system OS/2 was devised jointly by IBM and Microsoft to exploit some of the specific features of the 80286 microprocessor.

The 16-bit Intel 8086 and 80286 microprocessors helped establish a standard, compatible microprocessor architecture for the PC and gave rise to the massive installed base of compatible software. However, the arrival in 1985 of the 32-bit Intel386 microprocessor represented a major milestone in the development of the PC.

32-Bit Architecture

The i386, like the 80286 before, was designed to be 100% compatible with the existing MS-DOS installed base of software (and any other 286 specific applications, such as 1.x versions of OS/2).

One of the key benefits of the i386 microprocessor architecture is its higher performance. This high performance stems largely from the fact that i386 CPUs are able to process data and instructions 32-bits at a time, double that of the 8086 and 80286.

The i386 microprocessor also has very sophisticated memory management capabilities that enable users to run larger, multiple applications faster, with more efficient use of memory than with previous microprocessors. It is able to run multiple applications because unlike previous generations of microprocessors, the i386 CPU has hardware multitasking support built in.

As we have already discussed, Microsoft Windows 3.0 is able to run in three modes: Real, Standard or 386 Enhanced, which allows the software to run on almost all Intel x86 personal computer platforms. Microsoft Windows 3.1 is able to run in two modes: Standard and 386 Enhanced whch requires an 80286 or above microprocessor.

However, users of an Intel386 microprocessor based personal computer gain a significant advantage over those with less powerful systems. Apart from running the rich graphical user interface of Windows more quickly and efficiently, the 386 Enhanced mode uses the powerful features of thc i386 microprocessor architecture. When Windows is run in this mode it provides two major benefits; enhanced memory usage and multitasking of MS-DOS applications.

Using the demand paging capability of the Intel386, users can set aside up to 16MB of protected memory, even when the system has only 2MB of real memory. The ability of Windows to efficiently swap applications to hard disk allows users to run much larger programs more efficiently than on 8086 or 80286 based systems. A virtual 8086 mode built into the i386 microprocessor allows the user to run multiple MS-DOS applications in separate windows.

The rest of this appendix describes individually each microprocessor in the Intel386 family that you will find available in personal computers.

THE Intel386 SX MICROPROCESSOR

The i386 SX CPU is designed for the cost-conscious entry level user. It includes the 32-bit internal architecture of the i386 CPU family with an external 16-bit bus. This means that data arrives at the SX in 16-bit pieces but is processed internally at a full 32-bits. The design of the SX keeps the cost of the processor low while providing its users with all the advantages of the i386 microprocessor family, i.e. the ability to run present and future 32-bit software as well as all earlier MS-DOS software, multi-tasking and compatibility with all future microprocessors in the i386 family. The Intel386 SX runs at 16 and 20Mhz.

THE Intel386 DX MICROPROCESSOR

The Intel386 DX is a full 32-bit version of the i386 Microprocessor family. It was the first of the Intel386 family to be announced and is the most common processor of the family in use at the moment. The i386 DX is designed for the more power conscious users. It runs at 16, 20, 25 and 33Mhz and is most commonly found in desktop personal computers.

THE Intel386 SL MICROPROCESSOR

The Intel386 SL is one of the newest members of the i386 family (launched in October 1990) and is targetted specifically at the portable computer market. It is a highly integrated microprocessor and dramatically reduces the number of chips needed to build a PC. The i386 SL incorporates sophisticated power management and data security functions which make it an excellent solution for use by PC manufacturers when designing powerful portable computers.

The Intel386 SL runs at 20Mhz and will undoubtedly usher in a new age of laptop and notebook PCs combining all the benefits of the i386 architecture, together with true portability.

THE Intel486 SX MICROPROCESSOR

Introduced in April 1991, the Intel486 SX is an entry level version of the i486 DX CPU. It runs at both 20Mhz and 25Mhz and offers up to 40% higher performance than a similarly configured PC based on an Intel386 microprocessor running at 33Mhz. It therefore fills the performance gap between the Intel486 DX 25Mhz CPU and the Intel386 DX 33Mhz CPU.

The Intel486 SX differs from the i486 DX in that it does not include math co-processor support on chip, has a lower clock frequency and supports lower frequency peripherals.

As it is designed to allow users cheaper entry into the world of sophisticated and highly optimised 32-bit instruction microprocessors an upgrade is available that allows users to increase the performance of their computer system.

The first of these upgrades is called the Intel487 SX math co-processor and adding this to a suitable i486 SX CPU based system can produce up to a five fold increase in performance when running math-intensive applications such as spreadsheets and CAD packages.

When you purchase a PC based on any i486 CPU you should make sure that the system you buy is equipped with a performance or processor upgrade socket. Intel has been working with its OEMs in order that the specified (empty) socket is built into every i486 microprocessor based system. This ensures that users can easily upgrade their systems if they wish to do so. Note that the upgrade is not just limited to the Intel487 SX math co-processor. Soon, other

Intel performance upgrade products will be made available, offering users significant performance increases for a low cost.

THE Intel486 DX MICROPROCESSOR

The i486 DX is the most powerful of the Intel386 family. The i486 DX CPU brings mainframe type performance to the desktop - at a clock speed of 50Mhz it runs at a staggering 41 MIPS (that is integer performance of 41 V1.1 Dhrystones Millions of Instructions per Second). It is completely compatible with all other Intel386 microprocessors and runs all software written for PC compatible systems.

It is highly optimised for 32-bit instructions and so it is an ideal choice for users wishing to move to later 32-bit versions of Windows. The Intel486 DX runs at 25, 33 and 50Mhz.

It is important to note that the i486 is an evolutionary, rather than a revolutionary, step forward. It is completely backward compatible with the architecture of the Intel386. Software written for the i386 CPU will run without modification on an i486 microprocessor. However if you were to take an i486 and an i386 running at the same clock speed (for example 25 or 33 Mhz), applications would execute 2 times faster on the i486.

There are three features of the i486 that are largely responsible for this faster execution:

(1) In order to force shorter data paths between components and hence to improve speed and throughput, the i486 integrates on a single chip what were previously separate components in i386 CPU based systems. A standard i486 processor consists of an 80386 processor, an 80387 math co-processor and 8K of cache memory.

(2) Intel have used a technique called pipelining to streamline the way instructions are executed in the i486. What this means is that the i486 does not have to complete the execution of one instruction before fetching more. As the pipeline can hold up to five instructions, a LOAD instruction on the i386 that would take four clock cycles takes only one on the i486.

(3) The data path between the 80387 and the 80386 on the i486 chip is 64-bits wide rather than the usual 32-bits wide, allowing much faster execution of math intensive applications.

There are several things to look out for when purchasing machines based on the i486 microprocessor. One of these is whether the PC has a second-level cache installed.

A cache is an area of high speed memory that holds data and code that is frequently being used. When a processor runs faster than its main memory can deliver data (like the i486) a cache improves performance dramatically. With this new Turbocache 486 a performance increase of up to 15 percent can be gained for all applications. The i486 already has an 8K cache built into it. The Turbocache module has been designed to increase the amount of memory available to the cache (and thus eliminate cache overflow).

Up to four Turbocache modules can be plugged into one i486. Each module consists of an Intel 82485 controller chip and either 64K or 128K of static RAM, providing a maximum of 512K of cache memory.

APPENDIX

B

PC MEMORY EXPLAINED

When IBM designed the original PC, they never imagined that the maximum 1MB of memory that the 8088 microprocessor can address would become a serious limitation. Most other desktop computers at that time ran an operating system called CP/M (Command Program for Microprocessors - written by Digital Research) which had access to only 64K of memory.

When the PC was launched, IBM were surprised by the demand for the machine and the uses to which it was being put. Users soon started to call for more speed, enhanced graphics and bigger hard disks. However the loudest of these calls was (and still is) '... more memory'.

The memory within an IBM compatible PC can be divided up into a number of different types. The microprocessor at the heart of your PC will determine which types of memory you can utilise. Figure B.1 lists the different types of PC memory and the hardware requirements for each.

The rest of this appendix offers a more detailed description of the different types of PC memory available.

MEMORY TYPE	REQUIREMENTS
Conventional memory	Available to all PCs irrespective of microprocessor type. Conventional memory is the memory between zero and 640K.
Upper memory	Available to all PCs irrespective of microprocessor type. Upper memory is the memory between 640K to 1MB.
High Memory Area	Available to PCs with an Intel 80286 or later microprocessor. The H.M.A. is the first 64K of extended memory.
Expanded memory	Available to all PCs irrespective of microprocessor type. PCs with Intel 80386 or later microprocessors usually emulate expanded memory by using extended memory. Expanded memory is 'paged' memory and can be up to 32MB's.
Extended memory	Available to PCs with an Intel 80286 or later microprocessor. Extended memory is the memory beyond 1MB and can be many megabytes in size.
Virtual memory	Available to PCs with an Intel 80386 or later microprocessor. Virtual memory is a term used to describe the ability of the microprocessor to use disk space as random access memory.

Figure B.1 Different types of PC memory.

CONVENTIONAL/LOWER MEMORY

All PCs which contain an Intel 80x86 microprocessor and can run MS-DOS or PC-DOS have conventional memory. Conventional memory is the memory between zero and 640K and is where DOS application programs run from. There is an area of memory within conventional memory which is of significance in IBM compatible PCs. The area, 64K in size, is known as segment zero and resides at address 0000:0000 - 0000:FFFF. Segment zero contains the CPU vector tables and the DOS and BIOS variables.

UPPER MEMORY

The upper memory area is the area of memory that resides between 640K and 1MB. The PC specification states that this area of memory should be used to locate the video RAM and BIOS ROM.

ADDRESS (DECIMAL)	CONTENTS
960K - 1023K	BIOS ROM.
896K - 959K	ROM cartridge space.
832K - 895K	ROM cartridge space.
768K - 831K	BIOS ROM.
704K - 767K	Video RAM.
640K - 703K	Video RAM.

Figure B.2 Memory allocation within the Upper Memory Area.

The memory map in figure B.2 is the default layout for an IBM compatible PC. The contents of the upper memory area on your PC may be different as the information stored is dependent on the hardware configuration of the PC.

Powerful memory management software such as 386Max, QEMM, MS-DOS 5.0 and DR-DOS 5.0 make intensive use of the upper memory area to free as much space in conventional memory. On many PCs there are tens of kilobytes within the upper memory area that lie unused. The memory management software seeks out this valuable resource and relocates DOS device drivers and utility programs from conventional to upper memory.

Unfortunately advanced memory management is not a facility that can be enjoyed by all PC owners. Nearly all the memory management software on the market can only be run on PCs with Intel386 or later microprocessors. There are exceptions to this: both MS-DOS 5.0 and DR-DOS 5.0 offer clever memory management facilities to owners of PCs with Intel 80286 microprocessors.

HIGH MEMORY AREA (H.M.A.)

The H.M.A. is the first 64K of extended memory and is available on PCs that have an Intel 80286 or later microprocessor with at least 1MB of extended memory installed.

The H.M.A. came into being when a bug was introduced into the 80286 microprocessor's emulation of the 8086 chip. The bug has been retained in the Intel386 and 80486 for compatibility, but the A20 address has been added to allow the feature to be turned on and off.

EXPANDED VERSUS EXTENDED MEMORY

Whether you choose to use expanded (EMS) or extended (XMS) memory will depend on the micrcoprocessor in your machine and the memory requirements of the software you are running. Many older applications are unaware of extended memory and require expanded memory to enhance their performance.

EXPANDED MEMORY (EMS)	EXTENDED MEMORY (XMS)
Requires memory manager	Requires memory manager.
Requires 64K page frame in upper memory.	No page frame required.
Accessed by CPU in real mode.	Accessed by CPU in protected mode.
DOS can address it.	DOS cannot address it.
Available for 8088/86/286/386/486.	Available for 80286/386/486.
Slow paging process to access it.	Fast direct addressing.

Figure B.3 Comparison of expanded and extended memory.

EXPANDED MEMORY

To answer the need for more memory, Lotus, Intel and Microsoft agreed on a standard way for all IBM compatible personal computers to access more memory. This method is known as the LIM EMS (or Lotus-Intel-Microsoft Expanded Memory Specification).

Expanded memory exists outside the conventional memory map (the first 640K) and is accessed by paging. What this actually means is that an area of 64K in upper memory is allocated as a 'frame' through which 16K pages are swapped by applications that are able to utilise the LIM EMS access protocol. To access LIM EMS a special program called an Expanded Memory Manager has to be installed. If you are using an expanded memory card the driver will be provided by the manufacturer.

PCs with an Intel386 or later microprocessor can emulate expanded memory in extended memory using another utility called an Expanded Memory Emulator (EMM). MS-DOS is supplied with an expanded memory emulator, EMM386.SYS up to version 4.01 of DOS and EMM386.EXE thereafter.

The name change to EMM386.EXE in MS-DOS 5.0 was done to signal the fact that the facilities provided by the expanded memory emulator have been enhanced not only to provide expanded memory, but also to manage all memory in the upper memory area.

EXTENDED MEMORY

The paging process involved with expanded memory soon became a limiting factor and a method of directly addressing more memory was required. When Intel launched the 80286 they provided a solution to this problem by increasing the addressing capabilities of the CPU from 1MB to 16MBs. The subsequent releases of the Intel386 and i486 microprocessors have increased this limit further to 4 GigaBytes.

The upper memory area we discussed previously is also extended memory. You may see PCs advertised as being equipped with 640K of conventional memory and 384K of extended. However, more normally extended memory is recognised as any memory existing beyond 1MB: remember expanded memory does not exist in the memory map of a PC and so does not fall into this category.

Extended memory has many advantages over expanded memory but the main one is performance. Application programs that can utilise extended memory (many of the more popular ones do) will run much quicker and be able to offer more functionality to their users.

As with expanded memory, the efficient use of extended memory is governed by a clever program called the Extended Memory Manager. The extended memory manager's job is to stop different programs from using the same area of extended memory at the same time. MS-DOS comes with its own extended memory management program called HIMEM.SYS. Other compatible operating systems and memory management software (e.g. 386Max) also come with their own utilities that perform similar operations.

VIRTUAL MEMORY

The Intel386 and i486 microprocessors have the ability to manage (and access) virtual memory (this is the demand paging capability of the i386 architecture). Virtual memory is a term used to describe a memory management technique where disk space is used to simulate physical RAM. Virtual memory has been available on mainframe computers for many years but is still a rather new feature in the area of PCs.

The benefit of virtual memory is that your PC has an almost limitless supply of memory available. It must be remembered however, that the performance of virtual memory can in no way match that of physical RAM. Microsoft Windows and OS/2 use virtual memory to increase the number of applications that each can run concurrently. However if they are using a lot of virtual memory, system performance can become abysmal and in such cases it is advisable to increase the amount of physical memory in your PC.

As a simple rule of thumb, when running Windows your PC should have 1MB for the operating system and 1MB thereafter for each application that is to be run concurrently. For example, a 4MB PC should be able to comfortably run the operating system and three good sized applications.

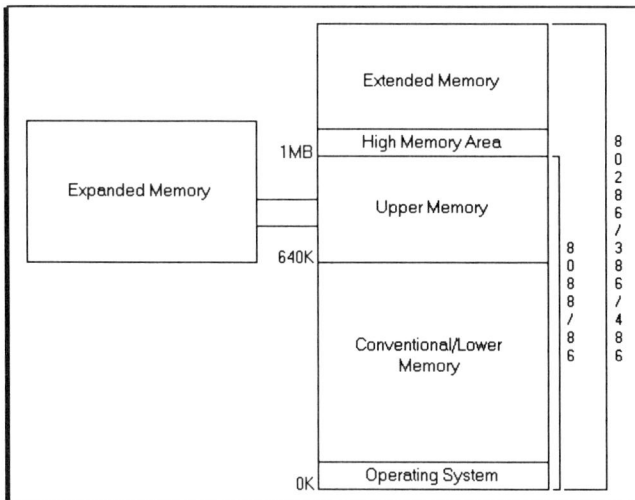

Figure B.4 Memory map showing all PC memory types.

APPENDIX

C

GOOD HOUSEKEEEPING

There are no definitive rules as to the way you should organise your hard disk and Windows desktop. However, by applying some common sense you can make your life and the lives of support staff a lot easier.

This appendix has been designed to give you a few guidelines.

HARD DISK ORGANISATION

A well structured hard disk will not only make your PC easier to use but can also increase performance. As an example, if you reduce the number of sub-directories in the root to a minimum, FILE MANAGER will load and run quicker!

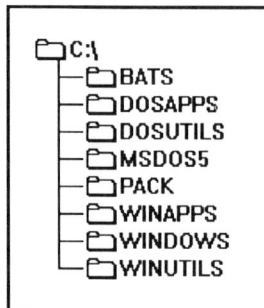

```
C:\
 ├─ BATS
 ├─ DOSAPPS
 ├─ DOSUTILS
 ├─ MSDOS5
 ├─ PACK
 ├─ WINAPPS
 ├─ WINDOWS
 └─ WINUTILS
```

Figure C.1 Example root directory organisation.

Figure C.1 is an example of a well organised root directory on a PC running Windows and MS-DOS 5.

Most of the directory names are self explanatory but so that you can get an idea of the principles involved, here is a brief description of each.

BATS   Holds all MS-DOS batch files, files that are suffixed with .BAT. You will need to ensure that this sub-directory is included in the PATH statement in the AUTOEXEC.BAT file.

DOSAPPS   Holds MS-DOS applications e.g. WordPerfect.

DOSUTILS   Holds MS-DOS utilities e.g. Norton Utilities.

MSDOS5   Holds the MS-DOS system files. If you are using a different version of MS-DOS then change the number on the end, e.g. for MS-DOS 3.3 name the sub-directory MSDOS3 and so on. The MSDOSx subdirectory needs to be included in the PATH statement in your AUTOEXEC.BAT file.

PACK   This is a special sub-directory which we include for those people who use file compaction utilities such as PKZIP. It provides an area of disk where files can be compressed and de-compressed without affecting other files on your hard disk.

WINAPPS   Like the DOSAPPS sub-directory WINAPPS is used to hold any Windows applications e.g. Excel and Visual BASIC.

WINDOWS   Holds Windows 3 system files and accessories.

WINUTILS   Like DOSUTILS sub-directory WINUTILS is
                 used to hold any Windows utilities e.g. Adobe
                 Type Manager and Microsoft Productivity
                 pack.

Obviously you may want to add to the above list. Do remember that
the more sub-directories you create in the root the longer it will take
the FILE MANAGER to count through them!

Carrying on with the above idea we also recommend that you create
further sub-directories within the WINDOWS sub-directory for each
of the Windows accessories that you use. For example, if you use
WRITE create a WRITE sub-directory, a NOTES sub-directory for
NOTEPAD and so on. Figure C.2 shows some of the sub-directories
that can be created within the WINDOWS sub-directory.

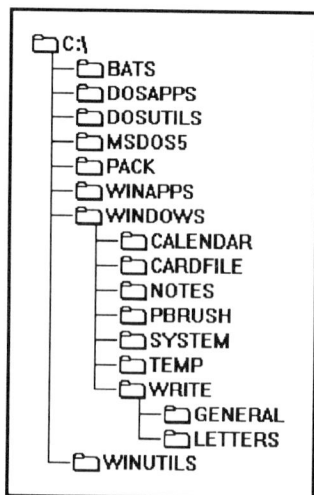

```
C:\
 ├─ BATS
 ├─ DOSAPPS
 ├─ DOSUTILS
 ├─ MSDOS5
 ├─ PACK
 ├─ WINAPPS
 ├─ WINDOWS
 │   ├─ CALENDAR
 │   ├─ CARDFILE
 │   ├─ NOTES
 │   ├─ PBRUSH
 │   ├─ SYSTEM
 │   ├─ TEMP
 │   └─ WRITE
 │       ├─ GENERAL
 │       └─ LETTERS
 └─ WINUTILS
```

Figure C.2 Example sub-directories under the WINDOWS sub-directory.

Windows is a very disk intensive application, reading from and writing to the disk constantly while it is running. This means that a large proportion of Windows performance is dependent on the speed of your hard disk. To see the amount of disk action that is taking place disable the SMARTDRV disk cache and watch the hard disk activity light on the front of your PC - busy isn't it!

As we have seen in previous chapters there are a number of ways to decrease the hard disk overhead to Windows: SMARTDRV is one way and using a ram disk to store temporary files is another. We also recommend that you purchase a disk reorganisation utility such as Speed Disk in Norton Utilities to optimise the layout of files on your hard disk. The disk reorganisation utilities will unfragment files, convert free space into contiguous disk space and sort the filenames into alphabetical order. All these features optimise the performance of your hard disk and should be carried out at least once a month.

MEMORY AND INTERRUPT SETTINGS

Many of today's PCs are unfortunately not plug in and go models and normally require configuration of both the software and hardware in order to do anything useful with them.

```
REM *****************************************************************
REM *                                                               *
REM * FILE        : CONFIG.SYS.                                      *
REM * DESCRIPTION : SYSTEM CONFIGURATION FILE.                       *
REM * AUTHOR      : PADDY COLEMAN.                                   *
REM * WRITTEN     : 6TH JULY 1991.                                   *
REM *                                                               *
REM * AMENDMENT HISTORY                                              *
REM *                                                               *
REM * DATE          WHO      DESCRIPTION OF MODIFICATION             *
REM *                                                               *
REM * 06/JUL/91    PADDY    FILE CREATED.                            *
REM * 17/AUG/91    PADDY    REDUCED SIZE OF SMARTDRV AND ADDED RAM DISK. *
REM * 01/SEP/91    PADDY    INCREASED SIZE OF RAM DISK TO 2MB.       *
REM *                                                               *
REM * HARDWARE SETUP                                                 *
REM *                                                               *
```

```
REM * MACHINE          : ZENITH MODEL 402-25 (486DX @ 25MHZ).        *
REM * MEMORY           : 12MB.                                       *
REM * VIDEO            : SUPER VGA WITH 1MB VIDEO RAM.               *
REM * HARD DISK        : 320MB (SCSI).                               *
REM * DRIVE A          : 3.5" (1.44MB).                              *
REM * DRIVE B          : 5.25" (1.22MB).                             *
REM * MOUSE            : MICROSOFT SERIAL.                           *
REM * DOS VERSION      : MICROSOFT 5.0                               *
REM * WINDOWS VERSION  : 3.00A                                       *
REM *                                                                *
REM * HARDWARE CARDS                                                 *
REM *                                                                *
REM * DCA IRMA-3           ADAPTOR ADDRESS 200-20F                   *
REM *                      PERSONALITY DCA/CUT                       *
REM *                      IRQ 10                                    *
REM *                                                                *
REM * 3COM ETHERLINK II    BASE ADDRESS C8000                       *
REM *                      IRQ 4                                     *
REM *                                                                *
REM * NEC CDR-75 CD-ROM    BASE ADDRESS D8000                       *
REM *                                                                *
REM * NOTES                                                          *
REM *                                                                *
REM * OTHER AVAILABLE UPPER MEMORY BLOCKS: E800-EF80,                *
REM *                                      F400-F57F,                *
REM *                                      FC80-FDFF.                *
REM *                                                                *
REM ****************************************************************

SHELL=C:\COMMAND.COM C:\ /P /E:2048
COUNTRY=044,,C:\MSDOS5\COUNTRY.SYS

DEVICE=C:\HIMEM.SYS /MACHINE:8
DEVICE=C:\MSDOS5\EMM386.EXE NOEMS I=B000-B7FF I=E800-EF80

DOS=HIGH,UMB

DEVICEHIGH=C:\MSDOS5\SMARTDRV.SYS 2048 2048
DEVICEHIGH=C:\DOSUTILS\MSMOUSE\MOUSE.SYS
DEVICEHIGH=C:\MSDOS5\RAMDRIVE.SYS 2048 /E
DEVICEHIGH=C:\MSDOS5\SETVER.EXE
DEVICEHIGH=C:\DOSUTILS\SCSI\NECCDR.SYS /D:NECCD /L:D /M:50 /V /E

BREAK=OFF
FILES=31
BUFFERS=1,1
STACKS=9,128
LASTDRIVE=D
FCBS=1

REM * END OF CONFIG.SYS FILE *
```

Figure C.3 Memory and Interrupt setting documented in a CONFIG.SYS file.

Once you start adding network cards, memory expansions, CD-ROM players, WORM drives etc. the whole business of configuration becomes quite complex. This is starting to change, and getting better, with the advent of computers based around EISA and MCA bus technologies (machines based around this architecture come complete with their own self-configuration utilities and do away almost completely with having to do any hardware configuration).

Whenever you or an engineer install an expansion card in your PC we strongly suggest that you take a note of any relevant settings and document them. Ideally you should lay out these configuration settings somewhere handy; we suggest you place them as REM statements in your CONFIG.SYS file as shown in the example in figure C.3. You should also take a printed copy of these settings and place it somewhere safe.

Version 5 of MS-DOS is the first version to support comment lines (REM statements) in the CONFIG.SYS file. If you are using MS-DOS 3.3 or 4 you should put the comments in the AUTOEXEC.BAT file.

PROGRAM MANAGER

Many users often forget, or do not realise, how easy it is to create new PROGRAM MANAGER groups, remove groups that they do not require and move icons and applications from one group to another.
The PROGRAM MANAGER shown in figure C.4 is just one example of a well laid out screen. You can see that groups such as Games and Accessories have been removed as they were not required. Some of the applications that normally appear in the Accessories group have been moved to the Main group.

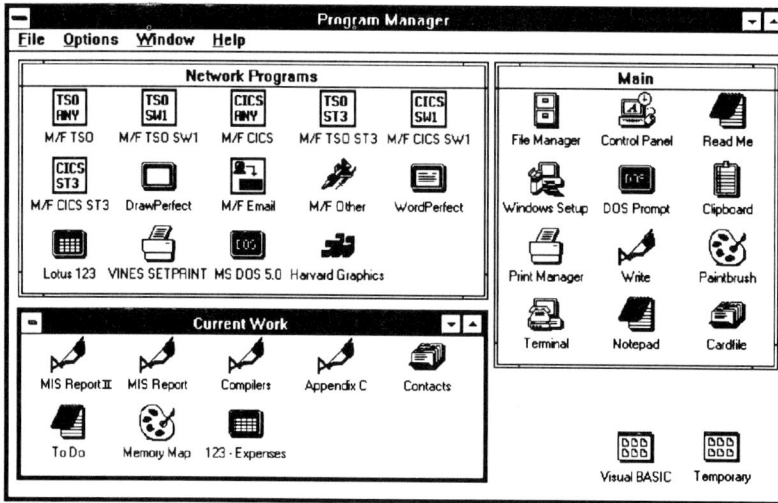

Figure C.4 A well laid out PROGRAM MANAGER using 800x600 Resolution.

Notice also the addition of a group entitled 'Current Work'. Creating such a group is often a good idea as it can be used for placing items that a user is regularly working on. As you can see each document has its own WRITE icon. This is achieved by entering the filename of the document in the PROPERTIES option in the PROGRAM MANAGER. Ensure also that an ASSOCIATION has been made in the FILE MANAGER between the file suffix WRI and the WRITE program.

MS-DOS BOOT DISKETTE

As we have seen, the modern PC is no simple beast; the configuration and maintenance are growing in complexity every day. Have you ever altered your CONFIG.SYS and/or AUTOEXEC.BAT file only to find that your machine locks up when you re-boot? A very simple way of protecting yourself is to create a boot (system) diskette for your PC containing the SYS.COM program and optionally default CONFIG.SYS and AUTOEXEC.BAT files.

The steps to create a boot diskette are as follows:

(1) Insert a blank disk in drive A and type.

```
FORMAT A: /S
```

The /S parameter informs MS-DOS to copy the system files COMMAND.COM, IO.SYS and MSDOS.SYS to the root directory of the disk in drive A.

(2) Next copy the MS-DOS AUTOEXEC.BAT and CONFIG.SYS files from the root directory of your hard disk to the boot disk in drive A.

```
COPY C:\AUTOEXEC.BAT A:\
COPY C:\CONFIG.SYS A:\
```

(3) Finally copy the SYS.COM program from your DOS directory on your hard disk to the boot disk in drive A.

```
COPY C:\DOS\SYS.COM A:\
```

The SYS.COM program can be used to copy the MS-DOS systems files back to your hard disk if necessary.

The next time you have a problem booting your machine simply insert the disk created previously in drive A and reset the computer (Control, Alt and Delete). You can then copy back the AUTOEXEC.BAT and CONFIG.SYS files if required or edit the ones in the root directory of your hard disk.

Finally remove the MS-DOS boot disk from drive A in your machine and re-boot the computer. If all has gone well the computer will at once boot into MS-DOS.

INDEX